Great Indian Chiefs

Great Indian Chiefs

by ALBERT ROLAND

CROWELL-COLLIER PRESS
COLLIER-MACMILLAN LIMITED, London

to Jo and the whole tribe

Library of Congress Catalog Card Number: AC 66-10552

The Macmillan Company
Collier-Macmillan Canada Ltd., Toronto, Ontario

Printed in the United States of America

THIRD PRINTING, 1969

Acknowledgments

꙰꙰꙰

THOUSANDS of books have been written about the American Indians over the past four and a half centuries. The few titles listed here were selected either because they provided background material and specific information for this book, or because they offer both an authoritative treatment of a subject and good reading. But such a limited listing can not acknowledge all the sources to which I am indebted, and I wish to apologize for the inadvertent omission of any book which may have provided inspiration or substantial factual detail.

Among recent general works on the American Indian, two excellent illustrated volumes present a comprehensive, vivid picture of the Indian world. One is *A Pictorial History of the American Indian*, by the late anthropologist and novelist Oliver La Farge, who aslo wrote the Pulitzer Prize-winning novel of Navaho life, *Laughing Boy*. The second is *The American Heritage Book of Indians*, lavishly illustrated and covering both North and South America; its editor, Alvin M. Josephy, Jr., is the author of *Patriot Chiefs*, a well documented and interestingly written series of portraits of Indian leaders.

Other useful general works on which I have drawn for the preparation of this volume are *Red Man's America*, by Ruth Murray Underhill, a clear and readable presentation of Indian history and culture; *Indians of the Americas*, a suggestive study ranging from the stone age to the mid-twentieth century, by John Collier, Commissioner of Indian Affairs from 1933 to 1945; *The Indian and the White Man*, a collection of documents selected and edited by Wilcomb E. Washburn so as to sketch the history of Indian-white relations since Columbus; *American Indians*, by William T. Hagan, a perceptive and concise history of the Indians in the context first of colonization and then of the growth of the United States; *Indian*

Art in America, by Frederick J. Dockstader, an authoritative and beautifully illustrated presentation of Indian arts and crafts.

For some of the chapters on individual Indian leaders, I am particularly indebted to Mr. Josephy's excellent *Patriot Chiefs* and to its extensive bibliography. Listed below are several good, readable biographies and a few, more comprehensive works which I found especially useful and which are suggested for further reading.

HIAWATHA: Thomas R. Henry, *Wilderness Messiah*; J.N.B. Hewitt, *Legend of the Founding of the Iroquois League*; Cadwallader Colden, *The History of the Five Nations of Canada*; Edmund Wilson, *Apologies to the Iroquois* (about the Iroquois of modern times). POWHATAN: Blair Niles, *The James*; George F. Willison, *Behold Virginia!*; Captain John Smith, *General History of Virginia*. PHILIP: Douglas Edward Leach, *Flintlock and Tomahawk*; Charles H. Lincoln, ed., *Narratives of the Indian Wars*. POPÉ: Charles Wilson Hackett, *Revolt of the Pueblo Indians of New Mexico*; Hubert H. Bancroft, *History of Arizona and New Mexico*. PONTIAC: Howard H. Peckham, *Pontiac and the Indian Uprising*; Francis Parkman, *The Conspiracy of Pontiac*; William Christie Macleod, *The American Indian Frontier*. MAQUINNA: John R. Jewitt, *The Adventures of John R. Jewitt*; Philip Drucker, *Indians of the Northwest Coast*. TECUMSEH: Glenn Tucker, *Tecumseh, Vision of Glory*; John M. Oskinson, *Tecumseh and His Times*. SEQUOYAH: Grant Foreman, *Sequoyah*; Marion L. Starkey, *The Cherokee Nation*. SITTING BULL: Stanley Vestal, *Sitting Bull*; Francis Parkman, *The Oregon Trail*.

My wife read the manuscript as it progressed, asking the kind of questions needed to steer it in the direction of clarity and historical accuracy. A friend, Stan Kelley of Princeton University's Department of Politics, served as a sounding board for the book in its formative stage. Neither is responsible for any errors of Indian history or politics. Thanks are due to family and friends who put up with my enthusiasms and frequent indignation as I retraced the lives of some great Indians and their peoples caught in the westward push of pioneers which made the American nation.

Contents

❦

1. The First Americans   1

2. Hiawatha and The Great Peace of the Iroquois   16

3. Powhatan, Emperor of the Indies   25

4. Philip of Pokanoket Fights for Freedom   35

5. Popé of the Pueblos: An Interlude of Victory   50

6. Pontiac, Friend of the French   63

7. Maquinna and the Traders of the Pacific Northwest 82

8. Tecumseh's Great Dream of Indian Unity   93

9. Sequoyah the Cherokee: The Magic of Learning   113

10. Sitting Bull and the Sioux' Last Stand   123

11. Indian Leaders Today   139

1

The First Americans

❧ ∼ ❧

THE INDIAN everyone knows is the hunter and warrior—
with feather bonnet and tomahawk—galloping bareback
after buffalo or sweeping down with bloodcurdling war cries
on a wagon train. Hollywood and television did not invent
these Indians. But insofar as their portrayal—much embroidered and often twisted—resembles historical facts, it ap-
plies only to some tribes living on the Great Plains between
the Mississippi Basin and the Rockies, and only to a period
of less than a century. Before the Spanish conquistadores
took over New Mexico the horse was unknown in America.
It was not until around 1750 that wild horses had multi-
plied in sufficient numbers on the Plains. Then tribe after
tribe took to them: Cheyenne, Blackfoot, and Arapaho; Co-
manche, Mandan, and Crow; and finally, the tribe destined
to fight the last and most famous battles on the Great Plains,
the Sioux. These Plains Indians have captured the imagination of millions, not just in the United States but the world
over. And yet they are but one group of tribes among many
hundreds; and their way of life, in which the horse was es-
sential, came into being long after colonization began.

But what were they like—the people who lived in what
is now the United States—when white men first arrived and
conquered their land? The answers are many, since there is

no such thing as *one* Indian culture. Languages were of radically different families, as far apart as English is from Russian, or French from Japanese. Physically, Indians ranged from very tall to quite short, from dark-skinned to ivory yellow—and many of the sunburned Europeans landing in the New World were far redder than the red man they met there. As for customs and ways of life, there was infinitely more in common between Elizabethan England and the Spain of King Philip than between, say, the southwestern Pueblos and the Indians of the Northeast.

The Northeast was a country of great woods and fertile land. Hunting and fishing were good, farming was easy even with the crude wooden hoes or pointed stones that were the only available tools. Men cleared the fields, then the women took over—planting, cultivating, and harvesting. Crops included some sixty kinds of beans, fifteen varieties of corn, and squashes.

Along the Atlantic coast, a number of tribes spoke languages belonging to the Algonkian family. This major language group took its name from the tribe of the Algonkins (or Algonquins, as spelled by the French) on the Ottawa River. Algonkian Indians on the eastern coast usually lived in dome-shaped wigwams made with frames of bent poles covered with bark or wooden mats. Villages tended to be rather small, as tribes broke up into several groups and settled where they found game. Chiefs were primarily war or hunting leaders, with little actual authority at other times, although even in their everyday pursuits men would listen to a chief known for great wisdom and experience. To the south, the influence of Gulf Coast Indians on Algonkian tribes brought about the development of more powerful chiefs and of larger organized units, such as Powhatan's confederacy in Virginia, which consisted of several tribes. (Powhatan was the father of the famous Pocahontas.) Generally, the Algonkian tribes on the coast were fairly peaceful. They received the first European settlers in a friendly manner, often provided them with food, and acquainted them with native crops and game, thus helping them make the difficult adjustment to a strange new world. It was only later, when caught between the colonists, who wanted more land, and the warlike tribes of the interior, that these Algonkian Indians rose up in arms and tried—valiantly but vainly—to save their country.

Most powerful among the traditional enemies of the Algonkians of the Northeast were the Iroquois, whose form of government was highly organized. Their villages were surrounded by sturdy wooden stockades, enclosing many long rectangular buildings with rounded or pitched roofs and covered with tree bark. Families of a clan lived together in one "longhouse," which had a central hall with a series of fires; on either side of each fire was a room which housed one family. The organization of the clans was based on descent through the women, who owned crops and houses. Although women did not actually rule, they chose the leaders; and if a chief did not live up to the expectations of the tribe the women could take from him the antlers that symbolized his authority.

Under the leadership of Hiawatha, some four hundred years ago, five tribes formed a league, called by the Iroquois The Great Peace, and later, by the early settlers, The Five Nations. As it grew stronger, the League expanded its power, often bringing in defeated enemy tribes as tribute-paying subordinate members. At the height of its influence, The Great Peace covered what are now the states of New York, New Jersey, Pennsylvania, Maryland, Ohio, Kentucky, West Virginia and northern Virginia, Tennessee—pushing west into parts of Indiana, Illinois, and Michigan, and north into Canada.

Iroquois support of the English played an important role

in breaking French power on this continent. If the League had fought on the side of France during the French and Indian War, England might have been defeated instead of gaining control of most of the continent. During the American Revolution, Iroquois warriors who fought for the British tied down considerable numbers of American fighting men. Notwithstanding the horrible tortures that were an inseparable part of Iroquois warfare—and the hatred they stirred in the revolutionary army—at the war's end George Washington concluded a just peace with the League. Their word thus pledged to the new nation, the Iroquois remained neutral in the War of 1812, depriving England of a powerful ally which might have made possible the conquest of the whole northern section of the United States, and bringing the war to a much less favorable conclusion.

The Southeast Indians never succeeded in creating the kind of tightly knit confederation which made the Iroquois so powerful. But the tribes which the first European explorers found living on the Gulf of Mexico had a highly developed social organization. Houses, sturdily built of wood, bark, and thatch were grouped around a council house and public square. Farmlands stretched sometimes for miles around, and here, too, the women did the farming. Each village or town was independent, though usually it didn't fight against towns of the same tribe and often joined with them against other tribes.

A head chief ruled the town. He had great authority, wore elaborate symbols of rank, and was accorded great honors. But he was made "King" by the will of the people, since high rank was not hereditary and could be gained only by proving superior fitness. The concept of the noble savage, which was central to the democratic theory of Jean Jacques Rousseau— one of the men who inspired the French Revolution—was probably strongly influenced by reports of the southeastern Indians. And the colonists' early contacts with them provided exponents of democratic thought, in both Europe and the United States, with new and fruitful ideas about organizing society.

The subordination of the military to civilian authority, for example, which has become a cornerstone of U.S. government, was a basic practice among the southeastern Indians. For even though they almost made a cult of warfare, war chiefs merely led the fighting; governing was left to rulers chosen for their wisdom and general ability.

The most famous tribes of the Southeast are the ones known as the Five Civilized Tribes: Creek, Chickasaw, Choctaw, Cherokee, and Seminole. These came closer than any other Indian groups to working out a new way of life and surviving on their homeland as full equals of the white colonists. They began acquiring cattle, firearms, and plows; they learned the use of the spinning wheel and other crafts. Traders frequently married into the tribe, hastening the adoption of European ways. For a time, contacts with the colonists helped the Five Tribes grow stronger and more prosperous. They were well on their way to proving that a relatively primitive people can learn rapidly from a more developed civilization and actually catch up to it within a few short years. In 1785 a treaty with the Cherokees recognized their progress by allowing them to send a representative to Congress—a right never exercised—and there was even talk of an Indian state in the Southeast being admitted to the Union.

The settler's desire for land and the westward expansion of a nation in the making did not allow the Five Tribes' development to come to full fruition. Groups of Creeks, Choctaws, and Cherokees already had been moving west of the Mississippi, anticipating the forced migration that was to come. In 1830 a law authorized the purchase of Indian lands and the removal of Indians at government expense; in the following decade, most of the people of the Five Tribes were moved to Oklahoma, under conditions which ranged from difficult to tragic. Those who did not die fighting for their native land, and who survived the long trek west, began rebuilding communities in Oklahoma and continued their abruptly disrupted development. In 1866 their support of the Confederacy resulted in a punitive treaty depriving them of half of the Indian Territory. However, the Five Civilized Tribes once again faced the threatened disruption of their lives with resourcefulness. The census of 1890 counted more than 51,000 of them, and in 1901 they became American citizens. When the Oklahoma territory became a state in 1907, tribal governments were dissolved, and since then the Indians there have become fully integrated; they hold public office and have a strong voice through their votes. Their children attend public schools, and a good number of them go on to college, so that many from the Five Tribes have become doctors, lawyers, and businessmen.

The Southwest, where Coronado, marching up from Mexico City, looked for cities with gold-paved streets, was an Indian world all its own. Rugged canyons and flat-topped mesas resemble a kind of lunar landscape. There are few rivers, but when it rains, water rushes suddenly down the arroyos, the strange creeks of the desert country that are dry and dusty most of the year. It is here that farming reached its highest point of development in North America before the coming of the white man. Unlike the Iroquois and the southeastern Indians, the men of the Southwest tribes did the heavy, endless work of farming in dry country. The women stayed home, and their relative leisure gave rise to highly refined basketry and pottery.

The Southwest Indians considered war a distraction from

the serious pursuits of agriculture, since it took strong young men away from the fields. Human sacrifice and torture were almost unknown, and when fighting was necessary to defend the village any warrior who happened to kill an enemy had to cleanse his soul through an elaborate ritual of purification.

Best known among the long-settled tribes of the Southwest are the Pueblos, so named by the Spanish because they lived in pueblos—villages or towns. Pueblo villages somewhat resemble a compact medieval town, with sturdy adobe buildings several stories high. In the center of the village are the kivas, buildings that are used for religious services and as meeting places for the men. When the Spanish first arrived, the Pueblos had strongly organized governments. Civil and religious authority were tightly intertwined, and the priests were usually the town's leaders. Formal ceremonies highlighted every public occasion. The Pueblo dances, continued to this day, are actually dramatized prayers for rain, crops, or fertility. The dancers, often masked and colorfully costumed, go through a strictly disciplined series of steps and gestures, to the accompaniment of human voices and drums. The ceremony has a religious intensity and a moving beauty. Sound, motion, and colors merge into a shared hymn of joy and communion with nature. Now, whenever the dances are publicly held, they draw people from all over the United States and abroad.

Living close to the Pueblos—and trading with them and raiding them in turn—were the Navahos, one of several tribes first known to the Spanish as Apaches (meaning *enemies* in an Indian dialect). The Navahos learned farming and weaving from the Pueblos. They also borrowed heavily from their rituals and mythology, producing exceedingly beautiful chants, at once poems and prayers, sung by the community led by priests. But the Navahos had no liking for the close-knit society of the Pueblos. Whatever they borrowed was adapted to their individualistic way of life, which found expression even in their shelters—the round hogans sometimes clustered to house a few related families but never gathered to form a village, and often isolated standing on a great empty stretch of land. Known for centuries as warlike raiders, the Navahos never were farmers on the same scale as the Pueblos. After the Spaniards arrived, they became sheepherders, silversmiths, and weavers. Navaho blankets and jewelry, both justly famous, are still produced today.

The primary concern for the Navahos, and to a greater or lesser degree for most Indians of North America, was to keep in harmony with the forces of nature and with an omnipresent, impersonal God. Sickness was the outward sign of *disharmony*, and so Navaho ceremonies—including the famous sand paintings—all centered on healing and bringing the individual into harmony again with the universe.

On the Great Plains, the tough sod made farming impossible without modern steel plows. A few Indians roamed these vast grazing lands before the coming of the horse; they were nomads living in tents made of skins. They used dogs to pull their few possessions as they moved from place to place in quest of game. It was a harsh life, and hunting on foot barely provided enough food. Then in the mid-1700s the Sioux and other tribes took to horses and moved out to the plains. Buffalo hunting, which before had been sporadic and difficult, now made possible a satisfying way of life. Buffaloes were plentiful and provided many of the necessities of life. Buffalo meat was eaten fresh or dried or pounded and mixed with fat and dry berries into pemmican. Skins were made into bedding and robes, shields, bags, and coverings for the conical, movable tepees that had once been painstakingly swathed in tree bark. Bones were used for tools, sinew for sewing, horns for cups, and the Indians' colorful costumes

A Pueblo village in the Southwest

included painted hides, polished bone breastplates, and horned headgear.

Tribal organization among the Plains Indians was loose and democratic. Peace and order were maintained by the influence of public opinion rather than by any formal authority. Chiefs were chosen for their wisdom and courage, and were followed as long as they proved their ability and did not disregard the wishes of the tribe. Strict discipline was enforced only during buffalo hunts when a kind of police force restrained eager hunters from frightening the great herd away, and ensured efficient cooperation so as to provide the most food for the whole tribe.

All the property of these nomadic Indians traveled with them, bundled on the long tepee poles and dragged behind horses. There was no chance to accumulate material possessions, and little prestige was attached to them. The way to renown was through prowess in hunting, generosity, and courage in fighting. The greatest feat in war was to make a "coup" (the French word for a "blow") by touching a living, armed enemy with one's hand or at most with a stick. Killing was not in itself praiseworthy; in fact, if an enemy was shot, the warrior who first ran up and touched the body that was still surrounded by enemy tribesmen, won more praise than the man who had shot him. By and large, war was a game, and it usually had little of the cruelty and delight in inflicting torture typical of many eastern Indians. The important thing was always the individual exploit for glory's sake rather than any territorial gains or the furthering of tribal supremacy.

The Northwest's cool and humid coast is a long step away from the Great Plains. In between lay the Great Basin, whose rivers never reach the sea but flow to lakes or are lost in desert sands. Here lived the Ute, Shoshoni, and other tribes, who spent most of their time securing the basic necessities of

CULVER PICTURES, INC.

Buffalo provided the Plains Indians with many of the necessities of life—food, clothing and tools

life: hunting all available game and gathering everything edible that grew in that arid soil.

Compared with these conditions, life on the Pacific coast was one of luxury and ease: the sea and the many rivers provided abundant and varied food and hunting was fair. Tobacco, used for chewing and pipe smoking, was the only plant raised. But there were wild berries, and Indians ate the starchy roots of the camas, a plant of the lily family growing wild in parts of the Northwest.

The relative affluence of the Chinook Indians on the Columbia River, of the Nootka and Kwakiutl tribes to the north, and of the Tlingit tribes in Alaska, found expression in living habits of a lavishness not common among Indian tribes elsewhere. Cooking, for example, was highly refined, with a variety of recipes and many different methods including broiling, steaming in pits, or boiling in boxes and watertight baskets by using hot stones. Houses, arranged inside somewhat like the multi-family Iroquois longhouse, were very large and sturdily built from wooden planks, with massive carved pillars. These were often faced with a totem pole symbolically recording the owner's triumphs and rank—in many ways the equivalent of a heraldic crest. A man's place in the tribe was usually determined by birth, with different rights and pre-rogatives for chiefs, nobles, and commoners. Inheritance, a practice almost unknown among American Indians else-where, was quite important. A man could pass on to his sons not only material goods but also social rank, the exclusive right to a fishing area, and the right to practice a certain craft (such as whaling) or to perform a certain ritual.

If the economy of the Northwest relied on sea and rivers as an abundant source of food, wood was its second main-stay. Giant evergreens—and especially the cedar, far easier to work than the eastern elm and hickory—were used for nearly every purpose, from building houses and big, hol-lowed-out canoes to fashioning all manner of utensils. These Indians knew how to steam and bend wood and how to inlay shell, bone, and copper. Their painted carvings, which range from vividly representational to highly stylized, rank among the finest Indian art in North America. Their basketry was also highly developed, though not quite as fine as that of the California tribes to the south. Weaving was fairly advanced too, incorporating different patterns and several colors; the yarn was usually spun from cedar bark or from the wool of mountain goats. But the Northwest tribes never matched the beautiful tailoring of the Eskimos, their neighbors to the north, whose more primitive fish-oriented culture had, in many ways, influenced their own.

The heritage of the American Indian has been richly wo-ven into the fabric of American life. Thousands of Indian names dot America's map, such as the musical Mononga-

hela and Minnesota and Appalachian. Nearly half the
nation's states have taken their names from tribes—Massachusetts, Illinois, Missouri, Utah—or from other Indian words.
American speech has been enriched by words and expres-
sions borrowed from the Indians: caucus, toboggan, squaw,
totem, hickory, medicine man, going on the warpath, bury-
ing the hatchet, and a great many animal names such as
caribou and skunk. Even our diet today owes much to the
first Americans: maize and sweet potatoes, pumpkins and
peanuts, the clambake, succotash (which originally included
fish as well as corn and beans), the Pueblos' tortillas.

The influence of Indian culture on American society goes
even deeper. The fundamental democracy of most tribes—
especially the principle of government by consent of the governed, which was, in fact if not in theory, the basis for leadership among the great majority of Indians—seems to have
played a part in shaping America's political system and social structure. A more direct connection can be seen between
the American Constitution and The Great Peace of the
Iroquois. We know that many of the men who framed our
Constitution were familiar with the Iroquois League. It
seems reasonable that in developing a concept of centralized
Federal government they might have kept in mind the
League's distinction between foreign relations, a function of
the central council, and internal affairs which were left for
each member tribe to administer. And certainly, the successful existence of the League was a source of inspiration for
colonial leaders seeking to unite the people of their new
country. "It would be a very strange thing," said Benjamin
Franklin in 1751, "if six nations of ignorant savages should
be capable of forming a scheme for such union, and be able
to execute it in such a manner as that it has subsisted ages
and appears indissoluble; and yet that a like union should be
impracticable for ten or a dozen English colonies."

The more we learn about the many cultures of Indian

tribes in different parts of North America the less Franklin's patronizing term—"ignorant savages"—seems appropriate. The Indians were different from the colonists, without a doubt. Materially, they were less advanced, and they did not have a written language. And yet there were budding centers of civilization that might have flowered: the industrious, peaceful Pueblos, for instance, had already gone a long way; given time, the democratic but aggressive Iroquois might have built another Roman Empire. But the white men came. Hunters, fishermen, or farmers, nomadic raiders or peaceful villagers, all Indians found their traditional ways of life challenged, then profoundly shaken, and finally irretrievably shattered. Except for the early days when Algonkian chiefs like Powhatan and Massasoit allowed—and often helped— English colonists to settle on the Atlantic coast, the history of the American Indians during nearly three centuries is a tragic one of defeat and enforced retreat, with a few bright but brief interludes of victory.

Through the lives of some of their chiefs—from Hiawatha who founded The Great Peace not long after Columbus discovered the New World, to Sitting Bull who led the Sioux during their desperate last stand on the Great Plains—we get glimpses of this history. There were many brave men, many wise statesmen. They tried to help their people and save their country, but the tide of settlers moving westward engulfed their lands. A new nation was founded. Eventually, the Indians who had been the first Americans began the difficult process of adjusting to the new America. That process is not completed yet. In some areas, their fellow Americans have been slow to accept them on an equal footing. Elsewhere, groups of the Indians themselves have refused to integrate themselves into the society around them, clinging to the old ways of life. But for the large majority, there has been in the last decades considerable progress. And once again, they have found brave and wise leaders to guide them. Without feather bonnet and without tomahawk, today's Indian leaders are professional people, politicians, artists, men of culture. On reservations or within the larger spectrum of American life, they make solid contributions to the present, and bring the rich gift of their past to that mixture of peoples and traditions and customs that is the United States.

2

Hiawatha
and The Great Peace
of the Iroquois

~~~~

THERE HAD BEEN no warning. Suddenly at dawn from the dark woods surrounding the village and its cornfields warriors rushed toward the wigwams with fierce war cries. They held sharp deerhorn-tipped javelins in their left hands, and swung heavy tomahawks with their right. Their faces were painted: some all black, some with black and red and blue rays on their cheeks, others with a wide black stripe across their eyelids or blue and black blotches on nose and cheeks.

The men of the Algonkian village, awakened by the enemies' cries, grabbed bows and arrows and tried to drive off the attackers. But the Iroquois, protected by corslets of bark or hardened deerskin, braved the shower of arrows and soon were inside the village. With javelin and tomahawk they killed all they met, warrior or woman or child. Before the sun had cleared the tops of the tallest trees in the east the fighting was over. The wigwams and the golden crop of corn were on fire, and the only village people left alive were those few who had managed to flee to the woods, and a few others who were prisoners.

The Iroquois party started back, stopping only long enough to draw on the side of a big oak tree, stripped of its bark, a record of their victorious expedition: little figures showing the number of scalps and prisoners taken, and of their own warriors wounded or killed. Their grey elm-bark canoes, hidden in the bushes by a stream, would take them back to their village.

Striking with merciless fury, the Iroquois had become the terror of their wigwam-dwelling neighbors in the Northeast. Along the St. Lawrence River, and throughout the forests of what is now the state of New York, the lands within reach of their stockaded villages were the scenes of bloody conflict. Nor did they wage war only against the various Algonkian tribes east and west of them, or against their cousins to the north, the Hurons. About the time Columbus landed in the New World, the Iroquois were constantly fighting among themselves as well: tribe against tribe, village against village, often clan against clan.

These were the people of the longhouse. Savage in war, they were a gentle people in their everyday life: kind to their children, generous in their hospitality, poetic in the magnificent legends they told and in their beautiful prayers to the Master of Life from whom all good things came.

There were five main Iroquois tribes in the Northeast. The Senecas, whose biggest settlement was on the shores of Lake Seneca, were the largest. The smallest tribe, the Cayugas, had only a few hundred people living in two or three villages. The other three were the Onondagas, "dwellers on the hill-tops," the Oneidas, "people of the standing rock," and the fierce "flint people" who were known to their enemies as Mohawks, or "eaters of men." (Cannibalism was rare even among the most savage tribes of North America, but it was often practiced for ritual purposes: by eating the heart of an enemy, warriors sought to acquire his courage.)

All of these Iroquois tribes were worn by decades of warfare, but warrior's honor demanded that the death of a relative or fellow tribesman be avenged by another death, in an endless cycle of blood. And pride forbade any one group to be first to propose peace, since this might be considered cowardly. There seemed to be no way to stop the constant strife —until out of the northern woods came a prophet, Degandawida, bringing a vision of peace and union among the tribes.

Hiawatha, a leader of the Onondagas, was one of the first to be won over. This real Hiawatha had little but the name in common with Longfellow's fanciful creation. He was a man, not a demigod given to tossing about mountaintops; he had a family, but had not romantically wooed and married Minnehaha; and he was most emphatically an Iroquois, not a hero of the Chippewas—the Algonkian tribe, traditional enemy of the Iroquois, from whose legends Longfellow borrowed most of the material for his poem.

Strong and brave, Hiawatha had long seen the folly of constant fighting, and had tried to find some honorable way to put an end to it. Many of his fellow leaders among the Onondagas were ready for peace, but all were afraid of Atotarho, a cruel and crafty chief who ruthlessly used murder and terror to maintain his hold over much of the Onondaga nation. Atotarho's spies kept close watch on Hiawatha's moves, and whenever he had gathered a group of chiefs and seemed nearing success in his drive toward peace, Atotarho and his men would appear, disrupt the meeting, and sow discord and fear. Atotarho would stop at nothing, and finally had Hiawatha's wife and seven daughters murdered. Grief-stricken and despairing, Hiawatha found only shallow sympathy among his fellow Onondagas, who were too fearful to openly defy Atotarho's power.

Going into exile to the land of the Mohawks, Hiawatha built himself a lodge of hemlock boughs in the forest, and lived the lonely life of a hermit. It was here, says the legend, that Degandawida found him. The prophet told Hiawatha of the dream which had started him on his mission. He had seen a giant spruce tree with five powerful roots to make it grow strong: the tree was mankind, and the roots the five Iroquois tribes. Together, these tribes would insure peace, represented in Degandawida's dream by a beautiful snow-white carpet stretching as far as the eye could see. Perching atop the tree, an eagle kept watch against any who might threaten The Great Peace.

Degandawida had been preaching his gospel of unity and peace to the Mohawks, finding many listeners in that war-weary tribe. He knew that Hiawatha could help him win over the Onondagas to his cause, and thus lay the foundation of a strong Iroquois alliance. Hiawatha was a gifted speaker and an astute statesman. He helped shape Degandawida's ideas into a practical plan for union, and going from village to village he became an enthusiastic spokesman for The Great Peace. More and more the people of the five tribes—warriors, chiefs, and women whose votes elected them—appeared ready to band together in the league Hiawatha advocated. The major obstacle remaining was Atotarho and the Onondagas under his power. Clinging to their old ways, they refused to join any alliance, and their killing and plundering forced the other Iroquois to fight back and thus prevented the establishment of peace and union.

Many legends are told of the cruel Atotarho, painted sometimes as a misshapen monster, with snakes instead of hair, fond of eating human flesh. Hiawatha finally went to see him, so goes one tale, and by singing the magical Six Songs gradually softened his heart, and then combed the snakes into human hair and straightened his crooked mind and twisted body. It is likely that the promise of a key post for himself—and a strong voice for his Onondagas—played

as important a part in Atotarho's conversion as the magic of
the Six Songs. But however this was brought about, it was
Hiawatha's triumph, and was followed soon afterward by
a solemn gathering of the leaders of the five tribes to found
The Great Peace. The League's council fire, it was decided,
would burn forever in the land of the Onondagas—and the
now peace-loving Atotarho would be its firekeeper.

The League's ruling council was composed of fifty chiefs,
selected by the women of the different clans as representatives. They served for life, unless removed from their office
for misbehavior or because of some serious physical handi-
cap. These chiefs could not be warriors (there were war
chiefs to handle military matters), lest their decisions be
warlike; in fact, if one of them killed a person—even in self-
defense or during a tribal war—he was immediately de-
posed. "The thickness of their skins," the League's constitution said of the chiefs, "shall be seven spans—which is to
say they shall be proof against anger, offensive actions, and
criticism. Their hearts shall be full of peace and good will,
and their minds filled with yearning for the welfare of the
people."

All the Europeans who came in contact with these leaders
were greatly impressed by their eloquence and wisdom. Father Hennepin, who traveled with the French explorer La
Salle, wrote, "The senators of Venice do not appear with a
graver countenance and do not speak with more majesty and
solidity than these old Iroquois."

The council met at least once every five years—more often
if any tribe brought up some important matter for discussion. The meetings were held at the chief Onondaga village, in a large bark-covered longhouse with a fire in the center as a symbol of the tribes' goodwill. Around the blazing
logs sat the fifty chiefs, wearing the deer antlers that were
their badge of office. Debates were conducted according to

Hiawatha, a gifted speaker and an astute statesman, established peace and unity among the Iroquois

carefully detailed rules laid down by Hiawatha and Degandawida in the League's constitution. The Mohawks and Senecas, who sat on the east side of the fire, first discussed the
matter at hand until they arrived at a decision, which they
then "threw across the fire" to the Oneidas and Cayugas for
their consideration. The Onondagas, who sat on the north
side, acted as referees, taking part in the discussion only
when the other two groups couldn't reach an agreement. After
a question had been thrown across the fire several times,
an unanimous decision would eventually be reached, and it
would represent the League's official stand.

In the decades that followed the formation of the League,
The Great Peace spread from the Iroquois strongholds of
central New York in every direction. Whenever tribes did
not embrace its principles and submit voluntarily to the wise
guidance of its federal council, the war captains of the five
nations enforced compliance. Instead of small raiding parties
typical of Indian warfare, the League could put in the field
armies of several hundred men, which no single tribe was
strong enough to resist. Thus the tomahawk enforced peace,
making the Iroquois masters of the Northeast. In the early
1700s, the Tuscaroras joined the League as the sixth nation,
and Iroquois power eventually reached south to Tennessee,
west to the Mississippi, and north well into Canada. Fierce in
combat, cruel in their treatment of those prisoners whom
they didn't want to adopt into one of their clans, the Iroquois
could be generous and statesmanlike toward the tribes they
had beaten into submission. The League's warriors protected
them from outside enemies, and as colonists began pushing
westward many groups of Indians asked for shelter in the land
of The Great Peace. If any internal difficulties arose, council
chiefs intervened to prevent strife and to help work out a
solution.

The Iroquois thus remained faithful to the ideals which

Degandawida had preached, and which inspired Hiawatha's work in organizing the League. These ideals were stated in three double sets: health of mind and body paired with peace among individuals and groups; individual righteousness paired with justice among peoples; strength for defense paired with "orenda," the spiritual power which pervaded all, and alone made a man or a nation capable of great achievements.

Translating these principles into concrete rules of conduct, Hiawatha succeeded in getting the League's tribes to adopt a series of laws protecting people's lives and their rights to liberty and to justice. One law, for instance, put an end to the custom of taking a life for a life, and established instead a compensation by the murderer due to the victim's family. Another law forbid cannibalism, although when fighting enemies of The Great Peace, warriors still might feast on the heart of a brave enemy, as a ritualistic way of absorbing his courage.

Once the Iroquois were united and the League's basic principles had been firmly established, Degandawida disappeared as mysteriously as he had come. A snow-white canoe took him across Lake Onondaga, says the legend, and away forever. But Hiawatha's task was not done. Turning missionary, he traveled forest trails and creeks and rivers to distant lands, spreading word of The Great Peace and exhorting other tribes to adopt its ideals. From the Delawares, from the Shawnees, from the Miamis on the western shore of Lake Michigan, back came messengers to the council fire in Onondaga country. They brought strings of wampum—many-colored beads, made from shells, which were arranged in designs telling of people who had sworn to live by the principles of The Great Peace.

Hiawatha grew old among his people, who loved and respected him and eagerly sought his advice. His wisdom and warm understanding of human problems became legendary. Statesman and legislator, missionary and counselor, Hiawatha in his later years started on still another venture. Realizing the importance of maintaining close contacts among the various Iroquois villages, he started what could be considered the first extensive road building program in North America. Trails were cleared, brush and trees and other obstacles were removed to open waterways for the heavy elm-bark canoes which were the Iroquois' chief means of transportation.

Long before white men ventured into the great forest wilderness of the Northeast, the Five Nations were progressing toward the establishment of an orderly world. The Iroquois couldn't write, but wampum strings recorded happenings and sealed agreements, and beautiful tales were handed down by word of mouth from generation to generation. They didn't know of the wheel and had only the crudest implements, but the rich soil yielded good crops and there was game in the forests and fish in the rivers to provide ample food. They could be ruthlessly cruel in war, but they were generous and kind in their everyday life—with laws to protect individual rights and to insure justice. The formerly hostile tribes had succeeded in forming a strong union, bound together not by the rule of a king but by a democratic constitution agreed upon by the representatives of tribes and clans. Different as it was from the kingdoms of Europe, The Great Peace held a promise of civilized development which time—and the newcomers' steel and gunpowder—did not allow to come to full flower. Its achievements within a brief span of history are a measure of Hiawatha's greatness as a leader of men.

3

Powhatan, Emperor of the Indies

⌘⌘

WRAPPED IN A great coonskin robe, with strings of gleaming pearls around his neck and a crown of feathers over his grey hair, Powhatan waited. The low platform on which he lay was covered with gaily colored mats and embroidered leather pillows, under a long arborlike wigwam made of wood and woven mats. Many warriors surrounded him, and brightly attired young women stood by the walls. Reclining on his elbow, with the majesty of one long used to being a ruler of men, Powhatan appeared deep in thought.

His brother Opekankano and his braves had taken prisoner one of the palefaces who had dared come up the Chickahominy River from Jamestown. He was now being led over a forest trail to the village of Weremocomoco, at the request of Powhatan, who was curious to see him. What did this white man want? Why had the palefaces settled at the mouth of the River James? Didn't they have a country of their own? They didn't seem able to grow or hunt enough food for themselves, and yet showed no desire to leave. On the contrary, they kept building more of their curious, rough-hewn wood cabins, and enlarging their village. Even women had begun arriving there, and from time to time another ship would bring more palefaces. What did they want?

Powhatan had heard of the palefaces before. He was sixty, and for many years stories had been told, of men with white skin and beards on their faces, with strange clothes and incredibly big ships, with sticks that made a bright flash and the noise of a thunderclap, and killed at a distance. But those men had always come and then left again. Sometimes they had bartered bright beads or sharp swords for food; other times they had killed many warriors and plundered a village. But until a group of English colonists had begun building Jamestown in 1607, Powhatan had not known of any palefaces settling on Indian land. Now, Jamestown was growing. Not only did its people appear determined to stay, but they were beginning to push inward, and even dared to venture into the very heart of Powhatan's country.

As the chief thought, he heard shouting and excited talk outside the wigwam. The crowd had sighted the war party returning with the prisoner. In a few minutes, he was bowing low before Powhatan. The chief looked over this strange creature with blue eyes and thick whiskers, who wore bedraggled breeches and leather jerkin, then bowed his head in return. Captain John Smith—that was the prisoner's name—stood waiting. Water was brought in to wash his hands, and a bunch of feathers to dry them. Then food and drink were served while Powhatan and his counselors debated the white man's fate. Should he be killed for coming as a foe to their country? Should he be treated as a guest, though uninvited, to avoid conflict with the palefaces?

A decision was finally reached, and Powhatan gave a command. Two Indians rolled a large stone in front of the chief, Captain Smith was forced to kneel down and place his head on it, then a warrior lifted his heavy club. Within seconds it would be over, but the adventurer who had braved all kinds of dangers even now did not flinch. And luck saved him just in time. Or, rather, it was a young girl, barely in her teens, who saved the Captain's life. Pocahontas was Powhatan's favorite daughter. Dressed in a soft doeskin robe, with a white plume in her jet-black hair, pretty Pocahontas had been watching the white man, admiring his courage before his captors and in the face of death. Now she begged her father to spare his life, according to the custom of many Indian tribes that a woman could claim a prisoner as her own. Powhatan hesitated, then granted her request. At first, he stipulated that the prisoner stay with the tribe and work for Pocahontas and for the chief himself, but a few days later he relented, and Captain Smith was freed and allowed to go back to Jamestown.

In the months that followed, Captain Smith returned several times to Weremocomoco. Powhatan's confederacy, which included many Algonkian tribes with some two hundred villages, was at the high point of its power. The weak, divided, and often starving community of Jamestown could not afford to fight it. In fact, since they didn't have enough food and needed corn, the colonists came to depend on the Indians for their very existence. It was good politics, therefore, to try to win their chief's friendship.

A ship from England brought special gifts: a bedstead with beautiful linen, a handsome pitcher and basin such as the nobility of the time used to wash in, and a glittering crown to be solemnly placed on Powhatan's head in the name of King James. Since the chief refused to travel to Jamestown to receive the presents, Captain Smith went once more to Weremocomoco, with another Jamestown leader. Carrying through the ceremony was not easy, for Powhatan was ill at ease and suspicious about the Englishmen's actions.

First, he didn't want to discard his mantle for a royal robe. Then, he refused to kneel, as was customary during a coronation, and it took Captain Smith's heavy hand to make him bow his head so that the crown could be placed on it. And at the gun salute closing the ceremony, the chief ran and took cover, sure that it was the signal for a treacherous attack by the white men.

Their splendid presents and an emperor's crown won the English some bushels of corn. But when they tried to secure the alliance of the Indians in fighting the Monacans, traditionally an enemy tribe, Powhatan refused. "I can avenge my own injuries," he told Captain Smith.

Even more disappointing to the English was the news the chief gave them that there was no great body of salt water beyond the mountains, no easy waterway to reach the Indies. Permanent as the Jamestown settlement was becoming, the colonists' chief aim was still to find a passage to the Indies. These were no Pilgrims in search of a country where they could live and worship as they pleased. It was the lure of a profitable trade, the hope of gold and silver that drew these first Englishmen to America, just as it had inspired Cortez and Pizzarro and Coronado.

When the dreams of quick riches did not materialize, the period of true colonization began. Women arrived, families settled in the New World, and the increasing population brought about more frequent incidents between whites and Indians. Powhatan's coronation had established fairly friendly relations, but not long after they cooled off. On a later visit by Captain Smith to Weremocomoco, Powhatan told him, "I have some doubts about the reason for your coming here. My men tell me you came not to trade but to invade and take over my country." The clash of interests between whites and Indians ran deep, and even affected their trade. Captain Smith wanted to barter trinkets for corn. Powhatan was ready to barter, and would give the colonists whatever corn was not indispensable to feeding his people—but he wanted guns and swords in return so that the Indians could, if necessary, fight the white men on even terms. Stubbornness on both sides finally brought the conflict out into the open, and sporadic fighting broke out.

Once again, luck and Pocahontas saved Captain Smith. The friendship the girl had formed with the Captain on their first meeting had since been cemented by several visits she had made to Jamestown—most of them without her father's knowledge. When she found out that Powhatan's warriors were to surprise Captain Smith and his men she went to warn them, and thus prevented a night ambush which might have dealt a death blow to the colony. Pocahontas' daring trek through the forest to alert the Englishmen went unnoticed by the Indians, but Powhatan suspected that her sympathies leaned toward the colonists, and later, when preparations for war began in earnest, he sent her to a neighboring tribe, the Potomacs.

A ship under the command of Captain Argall, another Jamestown leader, happened to sail upstream to trade with the Potomacs. When he heard that Pocahontas was there, he thought that capturing her would give the colonists a trump card in dealing with Powhatan. The promise of a shiny copper kettle won Captain Argall the help of an old Indian couple, who tricked Pocahontas into going aboard the ship with them. After a bountiful supper, the couple sneaked ashore with their kettle, while the girl was held on the ship and told she would be taken to Jamestown until her father would ransom her.

When a messenger told Powhatan the conditions for his daughter's freedom, the chief listened to him calmly, with a stony look on his face and without saying a word. He was to release a group of Englishmen he had recently captured, give back all weapons and tools taken from the colonists, and bring them a sizable supply of corn.

Powhatan told the messenger that he agreed to these terms. But he was in no hurry to comply, and let many weeks go by before taking any action. Should he give up the valuable guns and swords his men had succeeded in getting hold of? Would he be justified in weakening the position of his tribe by relinquishing the weapons? Much as he loved his daughter, his "delight and darling," Powhatan found the decision difficult to make. Finally, he released seven English prisoners and sent them to Jamestown with his promise of lifelong friendship—and of a large quantity of corn—if his daughter were returned to him.

"Your daughter shall be well treated," Captain Smith replied, "but until you send back our arms we will keep her here."

As time passed, Pocahontas grew quite accustomed to life among the colonists, and in turn was warmly accepted by them for her grace and charm. Before many months had gone by an English gentleman, John Rolfe—who had taken it upon himself to convert her to Christianity—fell in love with her and decided he wished to marry her.

Powhatan still refused to return the arms he had taken from the colonists. Safe in the great forests where the Indians not only outnumbered the English but could outmaneuver them by the favorite warfare tactics of sudden attack and fast retreat, he postponed meeting the English terms for a whole year. When he heard that Sir Thomas Dale, appointed governor of Virginia, was sailing upstream from Jamestown with a force of 150 men, the chief fled from Weremocomoco to a wilderness retreat. His warriors scornfully rejected the English request for the delivery of arms and prisoners, and fighting broke out causing much destruction in the Indian village.

Pocahontas, the daughter of Powhatan, was converted to Christianity by John Rolfe

Finally, a truce was arranged, and two of Powhatan's sons went to visit Pocahontas, who was on board Sir Thomas' boat. The news they brought back to Powhatan was such to gladden a father—and a chief. Not only was his daugher in excellent health and in good spirits, but one of the most respected gentlemen in Jamestown had asked her to marry him. Would Powhatan give his consent? He loved his daughter very much, and had missed her greatly. He would miss her even more, he well knew, once she married and settled permanently in Jamestown. And yet there was little hesitation in the chief's reply. The bond created by this union promised peace for his people—and Powhatan was too wise to overlook the power of guns and sharp swords and of the big ships that kept bringing more colonists and supplies to Jamestown.

A short time later—as spring of 1614 brought back to the beautiful Virginia forests the different greens of oak leaves and walnut and hickory, and the first flowers and wild fruits —Pocahontas and John Rolfe were married. The wedding in the little Jamestown church was a memorable event. There were English noblemen with their high starched collars and plumed hats, and laborers in rough, simple clothes. There were colorfully dressed Indian braves, including Pocahontas' two brothers and an old uncle who gave the bride away. Sieur de la Motte, a French knight, and Don Diego de Molina, a grandee of Spain, attended the wedding together with a few other Frenchmen and Spaniards who were prisoners of the English. Kneeling before the minister, Pocahontas repeated her marriage vows, speaking the new language hesitantly.

Powhatan had refused to go to Jamestown for the ceremony, for he still feared and mistrusted the colonists, and would not enter their town. But from that day on, he never waged war against the English, even though many of his counselors urged that the colonists' advance be stopped, and though incidents between Indians and whites kept occurring from time to time.

Only after Powhatan's death in 1618 did the tribes of his confederacy prepare for a major war effort to drive out the colonists. But the Great Massacre of 1622, a massive surprise attack which brought death to one quarter of the colony's population, came too late. By that time, the Virginia colony was too strong and well entrenched to be wiped out. It would have been possible—in fact, fairly easy—only fifteen years earlier. When the first Englishmen had landed and founded Jamestown in 1607, starvation and disease born of the surrounding swamplands had taken a terrible toll. And in the following years a determined drive by Powhatan's warriors could have stamped out the little community, weakened by lack of food and illness and internal dissensions.

Unlike the Iroquois, however, the Algonkians and the Southeastern Indians didn't use war as an organized effort to destroy another people or to conquer land. Fighting was very much a part of the Indian's life—a young man's way to prove himself and a warrior's road to fame. But the goal was to display skill, courage, physical prowess. Only later, when confronted with the continued expansion of the colonists, did the Indians begin to realize that this enemy was different from any tribe they had ever fought before. The English were not interested in war as an exciting game—a kind of bloodier version of the popular and rough Indian pastime of lacrosse. The English played for substantial stakes, for land and for the wealth to be gotten from it.

Powhatan may have dimly perceived this, but he thought that his people were strong enough to withstand the colonists' pressure, or that some kind of peaceful arrangement could be worked out, or that at least there would always be enough wilderness left to withdraw to and live just as his forefathers had. When Governor Dale—trying to strengthen the bonds established by the marriage of Pocahontas and John Rolfe—asked for the hand of Powhatan's younger daughter, the chief refused. Powhatan told Dale's envoy, "My country is large enough, and I would remove myself farther from you. . . . He cannot have my daughter. If he is not satisfied, I will move three days' journey from him and never see Englishmen more."

It was only a question of time. The chief's own son-in-law, John Rolfe, was beginning to raise tobacco, which soon became the colony's most profitable export. One after another, vast plantations were carved from great new hunks of Virginia wilderness. The world over which Powhatan had ruled, and where generations of Indians before him had lived, was coming to an end. One could think of that famous wedding in the Jamestown church as something of a landmark. Here was the daughter of the Emperor of the Indies marrying one of the enterprising and successful newcomers. She was brought to London and introduced as Lady Rebecca to the King and Queen of England. At this time the balance of power had not yet shifted in favor of the colonists, and white men and Indians dealt with each other as equals—bartering, seeking pledges of alliance, cementing peace with a marriage just as was done in Europe between heads of state. Soon the colonists would become the stronger, and begin pushing westward. One after another the free-roaming tribes along the whole Atlantic coast were faced with the choice between war and retreat. It would be two-and-a-half centuries before the close of the last chapter in the long tragic story of how the first Americans lost their country.

4

Philip of Pokanoket Fights for Freedom

❧❦

AT ONE END of the room sat the British Puritans, solemn in their dark suits, their hair cropped short. Their long faces were stern and full of ill-concealed hatred. Opposite them were King Philip and a group of his Wampanoag braves. Most of them tall and slim, they wore mantles of turkey feathers or squirrel skins over tan-colored buckskins. Flowing plumes or colorful beaded headdresses set off their long black hair. Proud and angry beneath a sullen outward calm, Philip and his men listened as a colonist listed the Puritans' grievances and charged that the Wampanoags were preparing for war.

When Philip's turn to answer came, the great chief arose. Erect and unflinching, he spoke of the land that had been his people's and that the British had taken over, tract by tract. He spoke of his father, the chief Massasoit, and of how he had befriended the first Pilgrims when they were few and lacked food. Were the Wampanoags preparing for war? True enough. But this was necessary, Philip explained, to defend themselves from the enemy tribe of Narragansetts.

The debate went on, charge meeting countercharge, and neither side yielded any ground. King Philip was a skillful diplomat, and although still young he had learned well how to argue with the British on behalf of his people's interests. Brave and proud, Philip had seen the Wampanoags—once masters of a large section of Massachusetts and Rhode Island —gradually lose much of their land. He knew the power of the colonists, and he knew that only a strong alliance of many tribes could possibly succeed in wresting the Indian land back. Until such an alliance could be fashioned, he must bide his time, and deal with the British so as to avoid a war for which he was not ready.

And so it was that on that spring day of 1671, after a long and heated debate in the Taunton meeting house, King Philip finally signed a treaty of friendship with the colonists. As pledge of peace he agreed to surrender his warriors' guns to the governor of Plymouth. Smarting under this humiliation, Philip and his men left Taunton and returned to Pokanoket, the main Wampanoag town, located on a peninsula jutting into Narragansett Bay.

It was fifty years almost to the day when the Wampanoags and the colonists had first come into contact, in the spring of 1621. The first winter in America had been harsh for the Pilgrims who had landed at Plymouth Rock in 1620. Great forests, unknown and frightening, surrounded their little settlement. Plymouth was just a village, with muddy streets and log cabins covered by thick thatched roofs. Food was running low, and the colonists lacked the wilderness skills that enabled the Indians to live in the dense northeastern woods.

One March day in 1621, a tall Indian wrapped in a rabbit skin cape, with feathers stuck in his long black hair, walked into Plymouth. The startled Pilgrims stared at the strange visitor who greeted them with the words, "Welcome, Englishmen. Welcome, Englishmen." He was Samoset, a chief of the Pemaquid Indians, who had learned a little Eng-

King Philip reluctantly signed a treaty of friendship with the British colonists in 1671

lish from some Maine fishermen. Samoset was a friend of Massasoit, chief of the Wampanoags who lived in the forests around Plymouth. Soon after this first visit, Samoset returned to the Pilgrim town with Massasoit and a group of Wampanoag braves. The British were few, and afraid that trouble might develop, so they prepared a royal welcome.

A trumpet and drum greeted Massasoit's arrival, and he was led to the newest cabin, decked out with cushions and a green rug spread out to cover the dirt floor. The British governor kissed Massasoit's hand as if he were a European king, and in the name of James I of England asked for a treaty of alliance with the Wampanoags. Massasoit promised that he would not let his people harm the colonists as long as he lived, and solemnly put his mark to the hastily drafted document. This allayed the fears of the new settlers and opened a long period of peaceful relations between his tribe and Plymouth Colony.

For forty years, until his death in 1661, Massasoit remained friendly to the English. It was one of his Wampanoag, Squanto, who taught the Pilgrims how to plant corn, putting a dead fish in each hillock to fertilize its growth. When visitors from Plymouth called on Massasoit in the Wampanoag town of Pokanoket, the Indian chief—handsomely dressed in a squirrel jacket and a mantle of turkey feathers—received them with great honors. It was Massasoit who in the late fall of 1621 provided four deer for the feast that was to be the first Thanksgiving in America. And many Wampanoags joined the colonists in the celebration. As a token of friendship, Massasoit's two older sons, Wamsutta and Metacom, were even given English names—Alexander and Philip.

Philip grew up like the other Indian youths in Pokanoket, living in a roughly built longhouse and learning the ways of the woods. He stalked deer, and soon could bag his quarry equally well with gun or with bow and arrow. Along the shore of Narragansett Bay were clams to be dug, scallops and fish to be caught. These provided a pleasant variation in the daily diet. The men hunted and fished, the women grew corn and beans in the garden plots. It was a free, satisfying life, which demanded a strong healthy body, a brave heart, and vast hunting grounds.

As the years went by, Philip saw changes taking place, and felt that they were threatening his people's way of life. The number of British settlers kept growing, and they were encroaching upon the Wampanoags' land. Some they acquired by bartering horses, guns, cloth, or other goods from Europe. Some they grabbed by threats or by tricking an unsuspecting Indian into signing it away.

No matter how a colonist had acquired the land, the Indians never understood why if the white man wasn't actually using it, they couldn't hunt there, or even raise corn. Philip's father, Massasoit, used his influence to maintain peace between Indians and colonists, but clashes still occurred which in time became more frequent. When Philip took up the colorful wampum belt that was the badge of chief of the Wampanoags, he knew that war must come.

"When the English first came here," he said, "they were few and hungry. My father fed them and helped them. Then more and more of them arrived, and they took from us tract after tract, so that we now have little land left. But I shall not live to be without country."

For thirteen years Philip waited. It wasn't in his nature to be patient, yet he restrained the young braves eager to strike back at the British. He traveled far and wide through the New England forests, talking to chiefs of other tribes and attempting to form a powerful alliance to regain control of their native land. Every time the British tried to interfere with Philip's negotiations, he met with the colonial authorities and managed to secure, through some concessions, another period of uneasy peace. He didn't want to begin war until enough tribes had joined the alliance, and a massive attack could be launched against all the settlements. Only this, Philip believed, could possibly succeed in freeing the Indians' country.

In June of 1675, however, events forced Philip's hand. One of his men, who had been educated by British missionaries and was serving as his secretary, betrayed his plans to the governor of Plymouth Colony. Soon after he was killed by fellow Indians. Three Wampanoags were arrested, tried, and condemned to death for this murder. Philip was enraged. In his eyes, the man's death was a just punishment for treason and no concern of the English. The Wampanoags were an independent tribe, and the colonial authorities themselves recognized King Philip as their ruler. What business did a Plymouth court have with internal tribal matters? Coming at a time when disagreements over land and other rights had created a tense situation, the hanging of three respected and widely known members of the tribe fanned the Wampanoags' anger and hatred against the British.

One sunny June day a small group of young braves, their tempers high, rushed into Swansea, the English settlement closest to Pokanoket. They were not in war paint but they acted treateningly and shot down some cattle. The colonists feared for their lives, and most of them fled from their homes to the garrison house. For several days the Wampanoags plundered the deserted village and roamed the countryside. At one settler's cabin, their bullying angered a young Englishman so much that he grabbed his gun and shot, wounding a Wampanoag. His comrades lifted the warrior on their shoulders and left, vowing vengeance. King Philip's war had begun.

Philip was not ready, but he had no choice. Blood had been shed, and his braves would wait no longer. Although his plans for a grand alliance of Indian tribes were not completed, and he had not wanted to strike at the British for at least another year, he knew that matters had gone too far. He had not chosen the timing, but now that the fighting had started he would lead his people, and hope that other tribes would rally to his cause.

Preparing for full-scale war, the Wampanoag women were sent west to the land of the Narragansetts, away from the scene of the immediate struggle. Messengers, wearing war paint and with rattlesnake skins on their backs, carried Philip's appeal for alliance. They went to the Sakonnets and their squaw sachem (or chief) Awoshonks. They went to the Pocassets, ruled by Weetamoo, widow of Philip's brother Alexander. They traveled through the wilderness of central Massachusetts to reach the powerful Nipmucks.

Philip's first concern was to gain the mainland, lest he and his warriors be trapped in the peninsula where Pokanoket was located. The colonists, hoping to prevent this move, hurried to ring the peninsula from the sea with a fleet of small boats, and assembled a force to march toward Pokanoket overland. But the Wampanoags had already escaped and established new headquarters in a swampy area on the mainland. All that the colonists found at Pokanoket were eight poles, each bearing the head of an Englishman. In revenge, the British trampled down the Indians' cornfields and burned their homes, leaving the Wampanoags' country a wasteland.

From the beginning, Philip proved to be a skillful leader, taking the initiative and keeping the colonial authorities off balance. Bands of Indians struck at Rehoboth, Taunton, and Middleborough in south-central Massachusetts, then at Dartmouth in the south. No one, in town or village or in a cabin in the woods, could sleep without fearing that the stillness of the early dawn might be broken by musket fire and the war whoops of the Indians. Philip seemed to be everywhere at once, and to the panic-stricken colonists he became the symbol of evil and doom, almost a demon out of hell. Rich rewards were promised for his head, and in hope of capturing him, a force of several hundred men was assembled to surround and attack his swamp headquarters.

To counter this maneuver, Philip sent some of his men to engage the British and draw them further into the swamp. When night fell, the colonists were deep in the wilderness, shooting at random, nearly lost. Many had been killed, many more were wounded, and the survivors realized the danger of their situation and beat a hasty retreat. There would be no further attempt to attack in the swamp; it was as dangerous, said one Englishman, as "fighting a wild beast in his own den." Instead, the colonists decided to cut off all possible retreat and force the Indians to surrender. They built a fort, they patrolled, and they waited, day after day. But Philip's men had been building canoes and rafts, and one moonless night they silently floated across the Taunton River and escaped.

The enraged colonists enlisted the help of a band of Connecticut Mohegans, eager to get scalps and booty from their traditional enemies, the Wampanoags. With this reinforcement, the colonists pursued Philip and caught up with him. But although he suffered some losses, once again Philip took refuge in a swamp and shook off the pursuers. Dividing his forces, Philip continued to march northwest toward the Nipmucks while his ally, Weetamoo, headed southwest to the Narragansett country with her Pocasset warriors.

News of the Wampanoags' successful uprising had encouraged some of the Nipmuck chiefs to go on the warpath. The authorities in Boston, still hoping to keep peace, sent a mission to negotiate. But as this group marched through the forest, single file, on a narrow and difficult path, a shower of bullets killed eight colonists. The survivors were pursued by the Nipmucks into Brookfield, a small frontier settlement of some eighty families.

At the cry of "Indians!" everyone fled to the garrison house, barely in time to escape from the war-painted Nipmucks who rushed into the town brandishing their blood-stained tomahawks. The cabins were plundered and burned, the garrison surrounded and repeatedly attacked. Finally, the Indians piled hemp, flax, and pine boughs into a cart, set it on fire, and by means of several long poles tied one to the other they pushed the flaming cart against the log wall of the building.

At just that moment, a detachment of forty dragoons arrived in Brookfield. Their unexpected charge dispersed the Indians, and the cart was hastily pulled away from the garrison house. To complete what must have seemed a miracle

HISTORICAL PICTURES SERVICE—CHICAGO

Colonists fled the town of Deerfield under attack by Philip and his Wampanoags.

to the colonists, a sudden rain storm helped put out the fire. Their lives thus spared, the people of Brookfield took a last look at the smouldering ruins of their town and fled east to safety under the protection of the dragoons.

The next day, Philip and his Wampanoags reached the Nipmucks' camp, and early in August their combined forces began an all-out attack in the Connecticut River Valley. Keeping the colonists guessing what his next target would be, Philip struck at town after town. Northfield and Deerfield were abandoned, most of Springfield was laid to ashes. And as troops rushed to defend a threatened garrison or to to escort supplies, they were often trapped and slaughtered in surprise attacks by the Indians, for whom the forest was home.

One bright fall day, a hundred-man expedition was ambushed while taking wagonloads of corn to Hadley. The party had reached a pleasant little stream where purple clusters hung from the grapevines festooning the trees on the banks. The captain in command let his men stop and gather grapes, putting down their guns. All at once—fierce war whoops, musket fire, and the Indians charged from every side. The soldiers tried to fight back, but they soon were in complete rout. Some tried to escape by climbing up trees and hiding in the branches. Indians spotting them, however, taunted them, dragged them down, and killed them. Few survived the massacre, and after that day the stream was called Bloody Brook.

The fighting continued through September and October. Cruelty was avenged with cruelty, and neither side gave quarter to the other. Scalping was common; both Indians and colonists practiced it with gruesome enthusiasm. Indian prisoners—women and children as well as warriors—were often sold as slaves and shipped to the West Indies or to Mediterranean countries. It was a merciless war because much was at stake. The colonists were determined to hold on to the homes they had built for themselves in the New World. And Philip knew that if the war were lost, the Indians' way of life could not survive. So each side fought on, stopping at nothing, killing and pillaging and burning.

When winter came, the Indians' food supplies were very low. Their stores of corn had been destroyed. The war appeared to drag on interminably to these people, for whom combat had always been a brief affair—often a single battle with an enemy tribe, after which peace returned. Many of the Indians could not understand why they should not stop, now that they had inflicted heavy losses on the English. But Philip knew that the only way to achieve victory was to wipe out all the colonists. He pleaded and argued, and succeeded in giving his men fresh courage.

Meanwhile, he was looking for new allies. In a number of meetings with Mohawk chiefs, he attempted to convince the powerful Iroquois that his cause was theirs too, and that union alone could safeguard the rights of all Indians. But the Mohawks, sure of their own strength, did not want to break off their profitable fur trade with the British, and they were none too eager to help the New England tribes, which were their traditional enemies.

Having failed with the Mohawks, Philip turned to the Narragansetts, in whose country Weetamoo's people and many of the Wampanoag women and children had been living. Philip found the Narragansetts more responsive to his pleading, although they had often been at war with the Wampanoags. But while their sympathies were on Philip's side, they were still hesitant. It was the British who unwittingly pushed them to take the last step toward war.

The colonies of Connecticut, Massachusetts, and Plymouth had decided to pool their forces and coordinate their war efforts against the Indians. After raising an army of a thousand men, they demanded that the Narragansett chief, Canonchet, turn over to them Weetamoo within ten days. When Canonchet ignored the demand, the colonist army marched against him.

The Narragansetts and Weetamoo's Pocassets, some three thousand strong, were entrenched in a village on high ground in the middle of a swamp. A log stockade surrounded it, with brush and fallen trees piled high on the outside. The only entrance was a narrow, well-concealed gap, reached by a secret trail that twisted through the tangled growth of the marsh.

Wary about venturing into the swamp wilderness, the colonist army camped a few miles away. While they were waiting, uncertain as to what they should do, a patrol captured an Indian who offered to guide them to the fort. On a bleak, freezing day in mid-December, they set off, single file, marching silently on the narrow path. Early in the afternoon they faced the brush-covered entrance to the village and began their attack.

Held off at first by fierce musket fire, the colonists charged again and again, and finally streamed through the breach. For three hours, savage fighting raged inside the village, and as the winter night set in, the English commander ordered, "Fire the wigwams!" Red bursts of flame and the wails of women and children added an eery horror to the battle. The Indians were running low on ammunition, and had suffered heavy losses; Canonchet decided to retreat.

More than six hundred Indians—men, women, and children—were killed that day. But a strong force of Narragansetts and Pocassets managed to escape through the swamp. The weary colonists, who had lost some fifty men and paid dearly for their victory, didn't even try to pursue them. Taking their dead and wounded, they straggled back to their camp, losing many by the wayside during the long night's march through ice and snow.

Late in January, Canonchet and Weetamoo joined forces with Philip in Nipmuck country. It was the largest Indian army ever assembled in New England, and the warriors were eager for revenge. From their camps in the central Massachusetts wilderness, war parties soon began to strike at towns in Massachusetts, Rhode Island, Plymouth Colony, and Connecticut. Sudden, devastating attacks at widely separate points forced the colonists to abandon town after town. Farmsteads and villages were burned, hundreds of families massacred. By the end of March a dozen settlements—out of some ninety in all New England—had been laid to ashes; about half the others had suffered crippling blows. The Wampanoags even marched into the capital, Plymouth, and set many houses on fire. It looked as if Philip's spring offensive might indeed succeed in driving the British out of the country.

The capture of Canonchet came as a rude jolt. The brave Narragansett chief was tracked down by Mohegans and Pequots accompanying a group of colonists, and taken prisoner to Stonington. Offered his life if he would try to stop the war, or help the British trap some of the Wampanoags, he refused scornfully. Condemned to death, his only comment was, "I shall die before my heart is soft or I have said anything unworthy of myself." Because of Canonchet's unswerving loyalty to Philip, the enraged colonists had his wife, children, and father murdered. Hundreds of Narragansetts were put to death, and after Canonchet was shot, his head was cut off and sent to Hartford as a gruesome trophy.

It was a tragic loss for Philip, who had found in Canonchet a faithful friend as well as a staunch ally. If he had not had doubts before, he must have wondered then whether the cause for which he fought justified the war's terrible toll. And was victory really possible? He had friends and loyal allies, but too many Indians had refused to join him, and others were now wavering in their determination.

There were those, like the Mohegans and the Pequots, who remembered ancient enmities and actually fought with the colonists against Philip. Others, concerned about their dwindling food supplies, were drifting away to find a hidden wilderness site and do their spring planting. Still others, despairing of ever wiping out the British settlers, thought they might make a separate peace and court British favor by helping them as guides if not as warriors. In rapid succession, a series of stunning blows followed Canonchet's death that weakened Philip's forces and turned the tide of war.

Through April and May, band after band of Indians was destroyed. No longer on the defensive, the colonists adopted Philip's tactics and with the help of Indian scouts struck swiftly and unexpectedly at camps in the wilderness. In June came another crushing blow. Awashonks, sachem of the Sakonnets, broke her alliance with Philip and a band of her warriors joined a group of colonist volunteers. A few weeks later, they tracked down Philip's secret headquarters and attacked him there. Well over a hundred Wampanoag warriors were killed or captured, and Philip had to make a hasty retreat, leaving behind the wampum belt that was the badge of chief. A more tragic personal loss was the capture of his wife and son, whom the colonists sold as slaves, shipping them to the West Indies.

Reverse followed reverse. Most of the Narragansetts were now disbanded, their best war chiefs dead. Growing numbers of Nipmucks were giving up the fight. Some joined the Mohegans in Connecticut, others surrendered to the colonists who showed them little mercy, hanging or selling most of them into slavery.

One of the remaining Nipmuck bands, hoping for better treatment, bound their valiant war leader, Matoonas, and delivered him to colonial authorities in Boston. Treason was also behind a surprise attack which led to the death of Weetamoo and the disbanding of her Pocassets.

Hunted from hiding place to hiding place, with no allies left, Philip began winding his way back to Pokanoket. Perhaps he knew he was going home to die, but he would not surrender. When one of his warriors suggested that he sue for peace, Philip angrily ordered him put to death. In revenge, the dead man's brother deserted and offered to lead a colonist unit to Philip's camp.

It was the night of August 11, 1676. Gliding quietly across the Taunton River, canoes took a band of forty Englishmen and Sakonnet turncoats to the southern end of the peninsula where war had started, a little over a year earlier. The traitor, Alderman, led them to the group of brush shelters where Philip and his men were sleeping. Creeping slowly, stealthily, the attackers surrounded the camp, some of the men ringing it closely and others forming a wider circle around it. At

dawn, a volley of bullets hit the camp. Philip and his warriors leaped up and raced toward the surrounding swamp—
only to meet the second ambush. It was Alderman's double-
barrelled gun that stopped Philip's flight: one bullet straight
to his heart and the second right above it. Thus a Wampanoag traitor killed his brave chief and put an end to the fighting.

Soon New England would be safe for the settlers, who
could resume their westward push. Settlement after settlement pushed back the wilderness, destroying the Indians'
hunting grounds and putting up fences where braves had
once roamed through vast green forests. Philip's war was
over. And over, too, was Philip's great dream of freedom
and independence for his people.

5

Popé of the Pueblos: An Interlude of Victory

꧁꧂

THE ROUND KIVA was dimly lit. The flickering light of a small fire brought to shadowy life the figures of kachinas, priests, and sacred animals painted on the curving adobe plaster walls. On one side of the room, a screen covered the dirt floor, to hide the opening to the underground world of spirits. In front of it, hushed and tense, a group of Pueblo chiefs and medicine men listened intently to Popé. As they watched in awe, Popé solemnly conjured up from behind the screen three masked, painted, feathered figures with fiery hands. Caudi, Tilini, and Tleume had come from the world of spirits to help the Pueblos wipe out the Spanish oppressors. The time for all-out revolt was at hand, they said, and all Spaniards must die or leave the country.

The Pueblos had had enough of Spanish rule. Coronado had first explored the Southwest in 1540, but only at the end of the century did the Spanish viceroy in Mexico decide that the lands to the north, where the Rio Grande flowed, should be added to Spain's great colonial empire. In 1598, Don

Juan de Onate marched into New Mexico, taking possession of the land "and all its native Indians" in the name of the king. His troops in metal and leather armor and high-domed helmets were accompanied by a group of Franciscan friars and by several hundred colonists. The conquest didn't take long. Brave as the Pueblos could be when defending their homes, they had no warlike tradition and were no match for the trained Spanish soldiers with their superior weapons and their horses, unknown to the Indians who regarded them as some kind of man-eating demons.

All through the seventeenth century, while on the Atlantic coast, the British, Dutch, and French alternately traded and fought with independent Indian tribes, Spanish rule laid heavy on the Pueblos. There were many dedicated churchmen truly concerned about the Indians' souls, and there were a few colonists who treated the people working for them in humane fashion. But on the whole, the Spanish colonial system was one of exploitation and oppression. The governor in Santa Fe exacted annual tributes, and people in every village had to give their fixed share of corn, woven goods, and labor. The priests worked to convert and baptize the natives, and put them to work building churches. The colonists used the Pueblos as a cheap and abundant supply of labor, and often the governor handed over a group of them, as serfs, to one of his favored friends, together with the land where they had lived as free men. Worst of all, from the Pueblos' standpoint, was the concerted action of church and state to wipe out all signs of the native religion.

Although large numbers of Indians embraced Christianity, many more did not. Even when outwardly Christianized, they held on to their age-old faith in the great living spirit that is everywhere, and in the kachinas, the spirits who are intermediaries between that god and men. Medicine men helped keep the ancient beliefs alive. No threats of floggings, jail, or even death succeeded in stamping out the ancient rituals, the elaborate kachina dances, or the customs handed down through generations.

One of the most influential medicine men was Popé, who, in the Pueblo village of San Juan, had long defied the Spaniards. To break Popé's stubborn resistance, his older brother was taken as a slave, and Popé himself was put in jail and whipped in the main plaza of Santa Fe. But punishments only strengthened his determination to defy his oppressors and lead his people back to their traditional way of life. Popé's influence spread from village to village, and at secret religious ceremonies the Indians listened in awe as he proclaimed that the gods were displeased and the friars and all Spaniards had to leave the Pueblo country. News of the unrest reached the governor in Santa Fe, and troops marched out to the Indian villages, bringing Popé and forty-six other medicine men back to the capital, where they were charged with sorcery and witchcraft. Three were hanged, as a warning, and the others were flogged and thrown in jail.

The Pueblos' reaction was swift and determined. Runners spread the news, and in village after village the people arose in anger, ready for joint action. A band of seventy Tewa warriors went to Santa Fe and demanded that the governor free the imprisoned medicine men. Faced with the possibility of a revolt—there were less than 2800 colonists in New Mexico against at least six times that many Indians—the governor let the medicine men go free. The threat of united action had won this victory for the Pueblos, and Popé left the Santa Fe jail determined to forge that unity into a weapon which would rid his land of the invaders once and for all. It was 1675, and for the next five years Popé patiently and carefully strengthened the ties among Pueblo leaders, fanning the people's hatred against the Spaniards and preparing for a general revolt.

The Pueblos continued their ancient rituals despite threats from their Spanish rulers

In the summer of 1680, Popé decided that the time had come. The meeting in the kiva at Taos was the last of many that had laid out in detail the plans for the uprising. On the same day, in each village, the Pueblos were to take up arms and kill all Spaniards. Then they would converge from all sides on Santa Fe and destroy the seat of Spanish power. Now all was ready, and only the date remained to be set. As the group of chiefs and medicine men watched spellbound, Caudi and Tilini and Tleume—their fiery hands throwing sparks in the dim chamber—told Popé to give the signal for the revolt by sending the Pueblos a knotted rope. The number of knots would indicate the days left before the date chosen for the uprising. The spirits disappeared behind the screen, and soon after, one by one, the men stepped up the ladder which led through a hatchway out of the underground kiva.

Next day, swift runners in relay carried the knotted rope of maguey fibers from village to village—Picuris and Tesuque and Pecos and Yugue-Yunque and all others. The revolt was to start on the eleventh of August. On the ninth, however, two of the rebel messengers were betrayed to the Spanish governor, who had them arrested in Tesuque. The news of this capture spread overnight to most of the Pueblos' northern villages. Deciding to carry out their plans immediately, so the Spaniards would have no time to prepare for defense, the Indians attacked. By day break on the tenth of August, the revolt had begun.

At Taos and Picuris, where well over a hundred Spaniards were living, only two soldiers managed to escape. The Pueblos and a tribe of Apache allies destroyed or sacked the haciendas and churches, then, under Popé's leadership, they marched south along the Rio Grande to join the Tewa Indians and go on together to Santa Fe. In the meantime, the Pueblos living in villages to the south and west, already free of Spanish rule, were converging on the capital. Armed with bows and arrows, lances and shields, and many weapons taken from soldiers and settlers, some five hundred Indians were waiting for the arrival of Popé and the northern Pueblos to begin their attack on Santa Fe.

Except for the governor's stronghold, the Rio Grande Valley from Taos to Isleta was in rebel hands. In two or three days, a colonial regime that had been firmly entrenched for over eighty years collapsed before the Indians' determined and concerted action. The settlers' haciendas and estancias were sacked, often destroyed, and cattle and horses were driven away. Churches were stripped of ornaments, and many of them were set afire. Some four hundred Spaniards were dead—settlers and their families, friars, soldiers. About a thousand others—men, women, and children—were gathered in Santa Fe, waiting anxious days and sleepless nights for an all-out attack. The rest, in flight to the south, congregated in Isleta and then—believing that they were the only survivors—marched on to safety in Mexico.

Popé's plan of action had proved successful so far. The Indians had freed most of New Mexico, and the revolt swept westward—to the sky city of Acoma, built atop a rocky mesa, and still further to the country of the Zunis and the Hopis. Pueblos from the south were already approaching the capital. Their leader was a Tanos called Juan. Riding horseback, he was armed with a Spanish harquebus (the first hand gun, actually a portable, muzzle-loading small cannon) and carried sword and dagger stuck in a sash of red taffeta he had taken from the convent of Galisteo. Juan was near the city when he was met by a Spanish patrol which asked him to enter Santa Fe and speak with the governor. Promised peace and forgiveness for all if the Indians would put down their arms, Juan answered Governor Otermin that there could be no peace until their plans were completely carried out. Otermin must choose between the two crosses the rebels had brought, Juan declared—the red one meant war, and the white one that all the remaining Spaniards would leave New Mexico forever. With these defiant words, Juan returned to the Indian encampment in nearby San Miguel, and was received with wild shouts and trumpet blasts and the ringing of bells. Soon after, flames and smoke rose high above the chapel of San Miguel.

The Spaniards, having failed to win peace through negotiation, had no choice but to fight, and Governor Otermin decided to attack before the arrival of the northern Pueblos. A furious battle raged on for many hours, and near sunset the Indians were forced to retreat. As Otermin's men were pursuing them, the Taos, Picuris, and Tewa Indians arrived at the north end of Santa Fe. The fresh warriors fought fiercely, and were soon lodged on a rise which dominated the governor's palace, firing harquebuses at the Spaniards who now found themselves under siege in the heart of the city. The outskirts were sacked and many houses set on fire.

Massed in strength, and surrounding the enemy from every side, the Pueblos were ready for their next move. They aimed their attack at the palace. After furious fighting, they succeeded in cutting off the ditch that supplied the palace with water, and their onslaught nearly gained them possession of the brass cannons at the gates of the palace. The Spaniards fought hard, trying vainly to regain the lost ground. The palace was without water. That night, Indian victory songs rang loud and wildly joyous in Santa Fe, as the Pueblos celebrated what they thought would be the imminent and successful conclusion of the siege.

The Spaniards' situation was indeed desperate. Without water, and with little food, there was no hope of holding out any longer. A council of war was held, and Governor Otermin and his advisers decided in favor of all-out battle—they would either die or break the siege. At dawn on the twentieth of August, the small garrison rushed out of the palace in a savage charge that took the Indians by surprise. Slashed by the Spanish swords, trampled by the horses' hoofs, the warriors around the palace were soon in flight. The Spaniards pressed this initial advantage and carried on the bitter fighting through the streets of Santa Fe. In a few hours, some three hundred Indians lay dead, forty seven others had been taken prisoner, and the rest were fleeing the city in disarray toward the surrounding hills.

It was a miracle, said the exultant Spaniards. And so indeed it seemed, for the five-day siege was broken and the small Spanish garrison had lost only five men while the Indians had sustained heavy casualties. Although the Pueblos were stronger in numbers with a hatred for the oppressors that gave them fierce courage, they lacked military organization and tactical training in warfare. Popé's leadership had kindled their enthusiasm and provided a well-thought-out over-all plan for the revolt, but it could not supply military skills which the Pueblos had not developed to the same degree as had the more warlike Indians, such as the Iroquois. For some eighty years, the Spaniards had kept them under tight control, forbidding them to have either guns or horses. Now, many of the Pueblos had gotten hold of both, but could not acquire the mastery of them which had made the Spanish soldiers the conquerors of an immense empire.

Whether it was because of superior military prowess, or the sheer force of desperation, or a miracle, Governor Otermin and his Spaniards had succeeded in routing the Pueblo rebels. They had water, now, and some food left behind by the Indians. But many were wounded, including Otermin, and miracle or not they decided that their wisest course would be to withdraw to Isleta, where they expected to join forces with the other survivors. The forty-seven prisoners were first interrogated, then shot in the plaza. Clothes and supplies from the governor's own hacienda were parceled out free of charge—with the secretary of government and war, Francisco Xavier, carefully recording in writing what was distributed. And the slow, long march south began, with women and children and the wounded—and few horses in any shape to be ridden. Smoke signals from rocky mesa tops along the route kept the Spaniards in constant fear of an attack, but although Indians were often sighted they did not give battle. Burned haciendas and empty villages were frequent reminders to the footsore and half-starving refugees of the collapse of Spanish rule, and when Governor Otermin reached Isleta and found it deserted, there was nothing left to do but retreat all the way to Mexico. By the end of September, all Spaniards who had survived the revolt were in El Paso, the ford in the Rio Grande which during the ensuing decade was to become a large and well-established community.

The Pueblos were masters of their own country once again. In Santa Fe, Popé vigorously set himself to the task of wiping out all signs of Spanish colonization. Christianity was the first target. The remaining churches and missions were either burned or converted to other uses, and all crosses and Christian symbols destroyed. To cleanse themselves of the friars' baptism, the Indians were told to bathe in the river and rub themselves with yucca suds and herbs. All Spanish names were abandoned, and the language itself banned. Timbers from churches and other buildings went into new kivas, kachina dances were regularly held, and the customs and ceremonies of the Pueblo ancestors re-established.

Popé's appeal for a complete return to the ancient religion and way of life struck a responsive chord in the hearts of most of his people. So eagerly did they "accept and embrace the commands of the first leader and captain-general, Popé," says a contemporary Spanish document, that a year after the revolt there was "not a sign of their ever having been Christians." It was another story, however, when Popé tried to make the Pueblos return to the past in other ways. He forbade the growing of any but the old native crops, for instance, and would have wiped out all that his people had learned from the Spaniards. But while Spanish rule was undoubtedly oppressive, it had brought about some progress. The friars had taught the Indians many skills, among them the making of adobe bricks in molds and the use of iron and steel tools. Along with the Spaniards had come several new crops—such as wheat and fruit trees—as well as wagons and more efficient farming methods. Now Popé wanted this useful new knowledge discarded, and with it the comforts of a richer material life.

Traveling from village to village, Popé sternly demanded compliance to his commands. Dressed in ceremonial garb, with a bull's horn on his forehead, he entered each village with the kind of fanfare that used to greet Governor Otermin's visits. As the Indians knelt before him, he would bestow on them his solemn blessing by scattering handfuls of cornmeal, and gradually he took on more and more of the outward appearances of the hated Spanish governor, even reserving for his personal use the old carriage of state. Faced with opposition, he threatened the vengeance of the gods on those who did not comply with his orders. And when opposition hardened, he began carrying out the gods' vengeance by ordering severe punishments and even putting people to death.

Spanish rule had meant the exploitation of the Pueblos by the Spanish governor. Popé soon was imposing heavy tributes, too. But while the Spaniards had at least been able to protect the Pueblos from the Apaches and the Navahos, Popé could not. In addition to paying him tributes, the Pueb-

los were forced to hand over to Apache and Navaho raiders
corn and cloth, cattle and horses. Conditions grew steadily
worse. Severe drought was followed by hunger and pesti-
lence, the Apache raiders became increasingly bolder and
more demanding, and Popé's fanaticism and tyrannic rule
fanned dissensions that led to actual clashes among Pueblos.

In El Paso, the Spaniards were biding their time, waiting
for an opportunity to reconquer New Mexico. They had
made a halfhearted attempt in the fall of 1681, when by order of the viceroy, Governor Otermin had marched north-
ward. But he had less than 150 men with him, and threatened
by the coming of winter and by a massive Indian attack he
soon withdrew. For the next dozen years, Spanish patrols
made sporadic attacks on the southern Pueblos, but only in
August, 1692, was a major attempt made to reconquer the
lost province. Skillfully combining a show of military force
with promises of complete pardon for any part played in the
rebellion, the newly appointed governor, Don Diego de Vargas, soon received statements of submission from most of the
villages. Much bitter fighting was still to come, but by this
time Popé was dead, and the unity which had won the Pueblos their independence had been lost in the clashes of rival
factions. Vargas played on Pueblo quarrels, gained allies,
and by the end of 1694 New Mexico was a Spanish colony
once more.

Popé had been a great leader. Rallying the Pueblos to the
cause of freedom, he had fanned their enthusiasm and led
them to victory. Had he led them forward from there, graft-
ing the newly learned skills unto their ancient traditions of
hard work, spiritual wholeness, and well-ordered community life, Pueblo civilization might have flowered under the
hot southwestern sun. The French and English colonies on
the east coast were still half a continent away, and weaken-

Apache attacks on Pueblo villages became more and more frequent

ing Spain might have found it too costly to fight a united and determined country. But Popé did not know how to preserve and strengthen the freedom he had won. In fact, he himself betrayed it by his pursuit of power and his impossible dream of stopping history. Progress may be a mixed blessing, but no people can have a taste of it and then return to the past. The Pueblos' opportunity was lost. A governor was back in Santa Fe, the friars and the colonists returned. Once again, the patient, sturdy Pueblos were put to work.

Their victory had been only a brief interlude.

6

Pontiac, Friend
of the French

❧ ❧

MAY 1, 1763, was a sunny Sunday in the Michigan woods country. Winter was over, and the Indians had returned to their villages after a hard winter of hunting and trapping. Trading the pelts they had brought back, they got clothing, supplies, and powder. The squaws planted corn, beans and peas, squash, pumpkins, melons; they mended torn clothes and repaired the cabins. The men and boys hunted and fished, and among their favorite pastimes were lacrosse and dancing. After a long and rather lonely winter, spring was a sociable time for the Indians. No one at Fort Detroit thought it strange that Pontiac and a group of his Ottawas from a nearby village should come one Sunday and offer to entertain the officers with a dance.

While the British watched the lithe young warriors who whirled and stamped and leapt in the Calumet Dance, a few of Pontiac's men slipped away and carefully observed the fort's arrangement and its defenses. The dance over, the Ottawas were served some bread, beer, and tobacco, and then left. Taking leave of Major Gladwin, the British fort's commander, Pontiac mentioned that as soon as the rest of his people came back from hunting, the Ottawas would all return for a goodwill visit.

Goodwill, however, could not have been farther from Pontiac's thoughts. His purpose was war and the capture of Fort Detroit, occupied by the British since 1760, when their victories over the French had given them possession of Canada. Now that Pontiac's men had gathered the information needed about the fort, he was ready to map out a plan of action, and he called a secret council of all the chiefs and warriors he had rallied to his cause. Gathered in a Potawatomi village two miles downstream from Fort Detroit, on the Detroit River, nearly five hundred Ottawas, Hurons, and Potawatomis listened to Pontiac's ringing and imperious voice stating once again his resolve to fight and drive out the British.

It is important, my brothers, that we exterminate from our land this nation, whose only aim is to destroy us. You and I can see that we no longer can supply our needs as we used to do with our brothers, the French. The British charge us twice as much as the French did, and their goods do not last. No sooner have we bought a blanket or some other clothing than we must get another. And when we leave for our winter camps they won't let us have anything on credit. When I visit the British chief and tell him that some of our comrades died, he doesn't express sorrow—as did our brothers the French—but instead makes fun of us. If I ask for something for our sick, he refuses and says that he has no use for us. It is clear from all this that they want to ruin us. My brothers, we must destroy them now. They are few, and we can win easily. All the nations that are our brothers attack them—shouldn't we strike? Are we not men like them? Have I not shown you the wampum belts I received from our Great Father, the King of France? He tells us to strike— shouldn't we listen to his words? What do we fear? The time has come. . . . After the British are defeated we will see what we should do, and we will bar every way that leads to our country so that they shall never return.

Tall and powerfully built, with the strong voice and the stirring manner of a great orator, Pontiac knew how to arouse the passions of his people. He stood proudly among

Pontiac envisioned a pact with the French to drive the British from Indian land

them, dressed in deerskin leggings and breechcloth, and a brightly colored shirt, with a few feathers tied in his black, straight hair. He wore silver bracelets, beads in his ear lobes, and a ceremonial stone through his pierced nose to ward off enemy spells.

A little over forty, Pontiac had grown up in an Ottawa village much like the one he now lived in: a stockade of stakes enclosing rows of long bark-covered cabins set in fairly regular streets. Like the Iroquois longhouse, each cabin housed several families, with sleeping platforms along the sides and a series of fires down the middle. As a boy, Pontiac learned the ways of the woods—hunting and trapping bear, beaver, buffalo, deer, fox, otter, racoon. The French traders in Detroit gave the Indians the supplies they needed in the fall, on credit, against the pelts they would bring in the next spring. The French commander at the fort followed the Indian custom of liberal gift giving as a token of esteem and friendship, and supplied the hunters with ammunition whenever they ran out and had no more pelts to trade. The French settlers living along the river near the fort were friendly and mixed freely with the Indians; they often spoke at least one native language, and liked to compete with the Indians in foot or canoe races. Many a Frenchman took an Indian wife.

While the British along the Atlantic coast were founding farm settlements, and kept pushing to get more land, the French were almost exclusively traders. Usually asking a tribe's permission before settling on its territory, they had established a chain of forts in the area east of the Mississippi, from the Great Lakes south to French Louisiana. Each fort had a small settlement around it, but the Indians considered this trading post as much for their own convenience as for that of the French. To the British colonists, however, this chain of forts meant a barrier to westward expansion, and conflict between the two powers over supremacy in North

America became inevitable. The first act was the French-English war of 1774–1748 (called King George's War in American history books). The fighting centered in the Northeast, with only a few minor engagements in the Great Lakes area where the French were firmly entrenched. Pontiac wasn't yet a well-known chief, but he took part in the action. Already a staunch friend of the French, he helped defend their fort against enemy tribes that had gone on the warpath at the instigation of the British.

Six years of uneasy peace followed King George's War, while both sides, well aware of their importance in the struggle for control of the continent, attempted to enlist the loyalties of the various Indian tribes. In 1754 fighting broke out again—the French and Indian War—two years before the outbreak in Europe of the Seven Years' War. The defeat of the French eventually made the British masters of North America. In one of the first major engagements, Pontiac's Ottawas contributed to the crushing defeat of General Braddock and his British and colonial troops (among whom, as a young staff officer, was George Washington). From then on, Pontiac himself took an active part in the French and Indian War. He fought against the British and against their Indian allies, the Iroquois and other tribes, until French Canada capitulated, and the Union Jack was hoisted at Fort Detroit in 1760. Many promises were made at that time by the British: that trade would be resumed and pelts would bring better prices; that they had no designs on Indian land; that they would show their appreciation of Indian friendship with presents and provide the services of a gunsmith and a physician at the fort.

British promises brought about a brief interlude of friendliness, but disappointment soon followed and by 1763 Pontiac was ready to set out on the warpath again. The basic issue, as it had been farther east, was land. The white man refused to recognize the hunter's right to his vast forest domain, and the Indian could not understand the white man's idea of individual property. The Indian belonged to the land, "our Mother," held in common by the tribe; no one man could sell it. Shared property was the Indian way of life, and this applied not only to land but to the other necessities of life; that was why Pontiac expected goods on credit if his tribe had no pelts to trade, and free ammunition when the men ran out and needed to go hunting.

General Amherst, however, who was in charge of the British forces in North America, had very firm ideas about gift giving. He warned his officers against "purchasing the good behavior of the Indians by presents," and especially against giving them ammunition. The old-fashioned British colonial attitude toward all "natives" was no help. Indians were to be disciplined if necessary, and otherwise ignored: officers and soldiers were not to mix with them. There was none of the easy friendliness of the French, who met the Indians on an equal footing and made an effort to learn their languages and customs.

Pontiac's list of grievances was long and real, and shared by many tribes. As he prepared to attack Fort Detroit, in May of 1763, Indians throughout the Great Lakes region and down the Ohio Valley were ready to join him—Miamis, Delawares, Shawnees, even the Senecas, notwithstanding their traditional Iroquois alliance with the British. Confident that the uprising would spread like wildfire once he took the initiative, Pontiac told his assembled warriors of the plan he had for capturing Fort Detroit. Two days hence, he would go with sixty men and ask for a council with Major Gladwin. All other Ottawas, women as well as men, would follow into the fort. Under their blankets—standard Indian apparel—they would hide tomahawks, knives, sawed-off muskets. When Pontiac gave the signal, they would attack the unsuspecting British. Meanwhile, the Huron and Potawatomi warriors would split into two bands: one to capture all English-

Pontiac and his warriors met with Major Gladwin at Fort Detroit

men outside the fort, the other to ambush any reinforcements that might sail up the Detroit River from Lake Erie and Fort Niagara.

On the morning of May 7, some three hundred Ottawas approached the fort—their gaily colored blankets draped over their shoulders or strapped around them. Entering the east gate, Pontiac noticed that twice as many sentinels as usual stood on guard, bayonets ready. Inside the fort, the shops were closed, all buildings had been locked up, and the whole garrison was lined up on the parade ground, fully armed. The British were obviously prepared for trouble, and Pontiac debated as he walked whether to risk the lives of his warriors now that a surprise attack was impossible.

Reaching the council house, Pontiac reproached Major Gladwin, saying, "We are greatly surprised, brother, at this unusual step thou has taken, to have all the soldiers under arms. . . . Some bad bird has given thee ill news of us . . . to stir thee up against thy brothers, the Indians." While talking with Gladwin, he held up a wampum belt—its white side facing the major and the opposite side, green, facing his Ottawas. He was to turn it around to give the signal for the attack—but he never did. After a few cautious and diplomatic exchanges, and many assurances of lasting friendship, the council broke up. Angry and confused, the Ottawas went back to their village.

Who had betrayed them? An attractive Chippewa squaw named Catherine, rumored to be in love with Gladwin, was the main suspect. Pontiac sent four warriors to take her to the major and ask him whether she was the "bad bird" who had made him suspicious of the Indians' friendship. Gladwin of course denied it, though he did say that an Indian had warned him—but Pontiac had Catherine flogged anyway, to set an example.

Now that the British were on their guard, it would be harder to devise a plan to get into the fort for a surprise attack. Pontiac first tried to reassure Gladwin of the tribe's friendly intentions, and then the Ottawas came to the fort for a general friendship council. This time, the chief had decided that even if the troops were ready the fighting would begin, but the Ottawas were stopped at the gate and told that only a few chiefs could enter. Pontiac angrily replied that all his people wanted to smell the peace pipe's smoke. If they were not allowed to, they would throw away the wampum belt the British had given them in token of friendship. The threat made Gladwin relent. The Ottawas could take turns, he said, and come into the fort in small groups. This would made an attack in force from inside the stockade impossible, and Pontiac stalked furiously away, followed by his men.

Back at the village, the chief didn't wait. Grabbing a tomahawk, he started the war song. They would attack now, he said, wipe out all Englishmen outside the fort, and keep the garrison surrounded until it surrendered. Before night, nine lives had been taken, and several prisoners brought back to the village. Messengers bearing war belts rushed to Indian tribes around the Great Lakes and down the Ohio Valley. Bands of allied Chippewas and Hurons won the first skirmishes, destroying a group of British soldiers away from Fort Detroit on a mission and capturing five boats carrying merchandise for the fort—including seventeen barrels of gunpowder. In rapid succession, surprise attacks were successful at Fort Sandusky in Northern Ohio, Fort St. Joseph near Lake Michigan, Fort Miami in Indiana—and in each case carefully planned treachery showed evidence of Pontiac's master mind. In addition to the Ottawas, Hurons, Potawatomis, and Chippewas, the Miamis were now also on the warpath. These were soon joined by the Delawares and Mingoes under Chief Wolfe, who massacred settlers in the Monongahela Valley and laid siege to Fort Pitt in Pennsylvania.

In less than three weeks, Pontiac and his allies had won control of a vast wilderness area, and the tide of war was running with the Indians. But at Fort Detroit, Major Gladwin had dug in and gave no sign of easy surrender.

The French settlers near the fort were torn between their dislike of the British and fear of the reprisals that might follow an Indian defeat. They were free to come and go between the fort and their homes, and many of them served as ambassadors or spies for either side. The Indians relied on the French community of more than five hundred traders and artisans for supplies and so Pontiac was careful not to antagonize them. He conscientiously paid them for requisitioned ammunition and provisions with birchbark I O U's marked with an otter, the sign of his clan. As the siege wore on, many Frenchmen grew worried about their situation, and a delegation visited Pontiac to complain of the Indian demands and of the overbearing way in which braves often acted.

Pontiac replied to the French, saying,

> My brothers, we never meant to harm you in any way, but among our young men, as among yours, there are some who always cause trouble no matter how hard we try to prevent it. Besides, I am not fighting the British for the mere sake of personal vengeance. It is for you, my brothers, as well as for us. . . . I don't ask for your help in fighting, since I know you cannot give it. I only ask for provisions for myself and my people. But if you wish to help me I would not refuse.

Promising that the settlers would have no more cause for complaint, Pontiac concluded his speech. His diplomatic reply not only showed his friendly intentions toward the French, but it made their concerns seem small indeed compared to the Indians' contribution to their own war effort. Pontiac shrewdly pointed out that though the settlers took no active part in this war, it was a common war that would end with the return of a French commander to Fort Detroit. There had been rumors of a peace between France and England, but Pontiac refused to believe them, and kept waiting for French help from Illinios. To hasten its arrival, he sent a message to the commander of Fort De Chartres asking for support against the British, in the hope that an officer would come and teach him how to conduct a truly effective siege.

This kind of warfare was new to him, but Pontiac knew that since the fort's defenses were strong, his best chance for victory was to starve out the garrison. Indian parties patrolled the environs, and lay in ambush along the waterways leading to it from the eastern posts. On May 28, they scored a major success. Ten flat-bottom boats on their way to the fort, carrying 96 men and 139 barrels of provisions, had

Indian parties ambushed British supply ships

been pulled up on the beach for the night. Suddenly Pontiac's warriors attacked and killed or captured over half the troops, taking eight of the boats and nearly all the barrels of food and ammunition. Rowing past Fort Detroit, whose garrison at first hailed what they thought were reinforcements, the Indians jeered and whooped in triumph.

A few days later, the Kickapoos, Mascoutens, and Weas around Fort Ouiatenon—in what is now Lafayette, Indiana —heard of Pontiac's successes from Ottawa messengers, and decided to go on the warpath. Inviting the fort commander to a council, they captured him with a few of his soldiers, and forced the rest of the small garrison to surrender. The prisoners were later handed over to the French at Fort De Chartres.

The next day, at the northern tip of the Michigan peninsula, a lively game of lacrosse between Chippewas and Sauks brought officers and soldiers out of Fort Michilimackinac to enjoy the exciting contest and the pleasant sunshine. Some Indian women strolled past the sentries at the open gates, and when one player hooked the ball over the stockade and into the fort, the Indians all rushed in after it. Dropping their lacrosse sticks, they grabbed the knives and tomahawks which their women had hidden under their blankets, and fell upon the garrison. It was one of the bloodiest triumphs of Pontiac's war.

In Pennsylvania, the Senecas broke from the Iroquois alliance with the British and went on the warpath. After destroying Fort Venango and Fort Le Boeuf, they joined a war party of two hundred braves sent by Pontiac and captured Fort Presqu' Isle. The Shawnees also entered the war, helping the Delawares and Mingoes who were besieging Fort Pitt. Numbering over three hundred men, the fort's garrison was strong enough to defend it, even though there had been an outbreak of smallpox. Two Delaware chiefs called on Captain Ecuyer and told him that the British forts to the north had been captured, and that he should abandon Fort Pitt before the arrival of a powerful Indian army already on its way there. The captain thanked them for their advice, and in turn urged the Delawares to bury the hatchet. When they left, he presented them with a gift of two blankets and a handkerchief—all taken from smallpox patients. The present achieved its intended effect, for a smallpox epidemic raged among the Delawares, Mingoes, and Shawnees for many months.

It was not the kind of war gentlemen had been used to waging in Europe. Treachery and ambush were Pontiac's favorite weapons, and the warriors who rallied to his cause often tortured prisoners or massacred women, children, and old people. Sometimes, contrary to the ancient tradition of Indian and white men alike, even ambassadors were seized and killed. Frenchmen usually escaped harm, but British settlers all along the western frontier of Pennsylvania, Maryland, and Virginia felt the full savage fury of the Indians. Men, women, children were butchered; cabins and barns were plundered, then burned. Many of the settlers were peaceful families who had worked hard to build themselves a home in the wilderness. Others were criminals who took advantage of the lawlessness of the frontier and often thrived by cheating the Indians. The braves on the warpath massacred indiscriminately.

In turn, the cruelty of Indian warfare aroused a blind hatred against them on the part of most settlers. The frontiersman was ready to believe that "only a dead Injun is a good Injun." And colonial militia bands often butchered whole villages as savagely as the most savage tribes.

Some British officers shared their view, and among these was General Amherst, commander-in-chief of British forces in North America. A brilliant military man, he had forced the French to surrender Canada—and was now bested by a "wretched enemy" whom he despised. His fury expressed itself in his orders to officers. Indian prisoners, he wrote Major Gladwin in Detroit, should "immediately be put to death, their extirpation being the only security for our future safety." His orders to another officer were to "take no prisoners, but put to death all that fall into your hands." And as an expedition was starting westward to relieve Fort Pitt, the general not only ordered Colonel Bouquet to take no prisoners, but also suggested that they contrive to "send the smallpox among the disaffected tribes of Indians." The idea was not original, since Captain Ecuyer had already tried it out, but it shows that—even though Pontiac and his allies were guilty of horrible atrocities—the British were hardly humane in their conduct of the war.

While Colonel Bouquet's troops were marching overland toward Fort Pitt, 260 men under Captain Dalyell had reached Fort Detroit by water, under cover of a heavy fog. Impulsive and ambitious, Dalyell dreamed of winning glory by defeating Pontiac, and managed to persuade Major Gladwin to let him try a surprise attack on the main Indian camp.

Before dawn on the 31st of July, Dalyell and 247 men filed out of the fort. Only the muffled tramping of feet and the occasional rattle of sabers and muskets broke the grim silence of the troops' march toward an enemy they thought was asleep and unsuspecting. But Pontiac was waiting. His French allies had told him of Dalyell's plans, and he was ready. After sending all women and children away from camp, he deployed 250 warriors to a wooded spot less than a mile from the fort, with orders to let the British pass. The rest of Pontiac's men were spread out in ambush around a narrow bridge over a creek, a mile farther upstream.

The British marched along the road in the bright moonlight. As the first platoon reached the bridge and started

crossing, a blaze of musket fire stopped them. The screams of
the wounded mixed with wild war whoops. Several soldiers
fell dead, but more rushed up and crossed the creek. They
dislodged the warriors hiding behind a ridge in front of the
bridge, but now Indians from the right and the left of the
main column began firing, creating confusion in the British
ranks. Firing soon broke out in the rear, and Dalyell seeing
that they had walked into a bloody trap, decided to retreat.
The Indians, however, were firmly entrenched in an exca-
vation dug for a Frenchman's new house and behind a
nearby pile of lumber. From there they controlled the road
and blocked the British retreat. After an hour of useless firing, Dalyell decided to storm the position, and bravely led
the charge. A bullet felled him, but his soldiers rushed past
his dead body and dislodged the Indians. The way to the fort
was now clear, and by eight in the morning the last of the
survivors was safely back. Twenty had been killed, forty-
two others were wounded—and the creek where Pontiac had
ambushed the British had gained a new name, Bloody Run.

Captain Dalyell's defeat and death increased Pontiac's
prestige and gave his warriors' morale a boost. But most of
the reinforcements Dalyell had brought to Fort Detroit were
still there to strengthen its garrison. A few days later, another
sixty men with supplies arrived from Fort Niagara. Meanwhile, Colonel Bouquet on his way to Fort Pitt had been engaged in battle by a strong force of Delawares, Mingoes,
Shawnees, and Hurons, and had put them to flight. His arrival at Fort Pitt broke the siege.

Stymied in their efforts to destroy the last two British
forts west of the Ohio River, the Indians changed fronts.
Pontiac was still determined to break up the supply line to
Detroit, and the next major attack took place near Fort Niagara. Supplies from the east coast were unloaded at the bottom of the falls; wagons carried them up a long, narrow

winding road to the top, and from there boats took them westward by way of Lake Erie. In mid-September, the Indians struck at such a wagon train, surprising the soldiers at a spot where the road ran between dense woods on one side and a yawning chasm on the other. There was no retreat for the British. Panicked horses and oxen plunged down, dragging soldiers to death with them. The first massive burst of musket fire was followed by a fierce charge of Indians, tomahawks in hand, and soon the fighting was over. Two companies rushing to the rescue were ambushed a mile away, and out of eighty men only a few managed to escape.

It was the last triumph of Pontiac's war. The fighting had lasted too long, and the Indians' need for food was getting stronger than their hatred for the British. Band after band of warriors took off in their canoes to hunt, and chiefs from different tribes held councils with Major Gladwin, offering to bury the hatchet. The French settlers, convinced by now that Pontiac could not win, began supplying the fort's garrison with much-needed wheat. Calling a grand council, Pontiac appealed for pursuing the war until victory would secure their country for the Indians and their French brothers. But his impassioned words couldn't change the hard facts. Winter was coming, and his people needed food and those goods they could get only from the white man's trade.

On October 29, it snowed. That same night, a French officer brought Pontiac a letter from the commander of Fort De Chartres. France and England, the letter said, had indeed made peace. It was the desire of the French king that his children—the Indian nations of the Great Lakes—bury the hatchet and smoke the peace pipe with the British. What could Pontiac do? There would be no help from the Illinois. His allies were deserting him, his leadership in his own tribe was questioned. With winter coming, he could not keep up the siege defying French opposition in addition to fighting Major Gladwin.

Pontiac began a note addressed to the Major:

> My brother, the word which my father has sent to make peace I have accepted. All my young men have buried their hatchets. I think you will forget the evil things which have been taking place now for some time. Likewise I shall forget what you may have done to me, in order to think of nothing but good. I, the Chippewas, the Hurons, we will speak with you whenever you ask us. Give us an answer. I am sending you this resolution so that you may see it. If you are as well-intentioned as I, you will answer me. I wish you a good day. Pontiac.

A month later, the chief left Detroit with a part of the Ottawa tribe still faithful to him. They spent the winter on the Maumee River, hoping to renew war when the good season returned. The Delawares and Shawnees had not buried the hatchet; the Senecas had attacked the British near Niagara as late as November; some Huron bands and the Miamis were still ready to fight. In the spring, Pontiac traveled south to visit the tribes along the Illinois and the French commander of Fort De Chartres. With ammunition from the French and the support of the Illinois nations, there was still hope that the British could be defeated.

Summer came, however, and Pontiac's war was not resumed. The main reason was lack of ammunition, which the French did not dare provide in fear of British reprisals. As the months went by, more of Pontiac's allies defected. In the fall, an expedition led by Colonel Bouquet forced the Delawares and Shawnees to sign a peace treaty. It was the end of Pontiac's hopes. In July, 1765, the chief formally bound himself to keep the peace. One condition he insisted on writing into the treaty was that British possession of former French forts did not carry with it the right for settlers to move in. The Indians had allowed the French to build forts and trading posts in their country; now they would allow the British to do so. But both French and British were only tenants—the country belonged to the Indians. The British representative assured the chief that this right would be respected, although he knew that England claimed ownership of the land. International justice and law did not apply when dealing with Indian nations.

Still influential among the tribes of the Great Lakes and the Illinois, Pontiac upheld his promise: "For the future we will regard the British as brothers." But his star was declining fast. At a peace congress in Oswego, New York, in 1766, Pontiac was the main spokesman for all the western nations. The British Indian agent, Sir William Johnson, showed him special consideration in order to fan the jealousies of the other chiefs, and rumors were spread that Pontiac, the leader of the war against the British, was now receiving a pension from them. From then on, even Pontiac's own people began to turn against him. He finally left his tribe, and with a few relatives and friends traveled to the Illinois country. One day, he visited a trade store near St. Louis with a Peoria Indian. When they came out and started down the street, the Peoria hit him with his club, stunning him, and then stabbed him to death, apparently in revenge of some earlier offense.

Pontiac fought a valiant war. He brought together eighteen powerful tribes, and his warriors defied and repeatedly defeated the forces of proud General Amherst. Over four hundred British soldiers and many hundreds of settlers were killed. British control over the wilderness from Lake Ontario to the Mississippi was broken. And yet, Pontiac's war was lost. The chief knew from the beginning that the Indians were not strong enough, by themselves, to banish the British from their country. French help was indispensable. Pontiac's dream was to preserve the Indian nations as sovereign allies of the French, who could establish settlements for mutually advantageous trade but who would not encroach on the wilderness hunting grounds. The defeat of the French doomed Pontiac's cause.

The British government never recognized the Indians' right to their own country, but Pontiac's war forced the British to try to find a solution which would prevent costly and bloody conflicts. In October, 1763, shortly before the Ottawa chief lifted his siege of Fort Detroit, a royal proclamation set the crest of the Appalachians as the western boundary of white settlement. The land beyond would remain Indian country. But an order from London could not stop the westward march of the settlers. British in name, they were now Americans. Before long, they would break away from England and become a new nation. And the United States of America would set aside the Appalachian boundary, as tide upon tide of pioneers surged westward engulfing the Indians' lands.

7

Maquinna and the Traders of the Pacific Northwest

～～

WHEN THE big ship sailed past the village on Friendly Cove, heading up the natural channel leading inland, Maquinna decided that the next morning he would follow it and pay the white men a visit. It was an occasion that didn't present itself often, and it called for special preparations. Early at dawn, the chief began his careful grooming, painting broad black stripes over his eyebrows, and small red squares over the rest of his face. His arms and legs were also painted red, and over his well-oiled black hair, gathered in a bunch atop his head, was strewn white eagle down. He wore a magnificent cloak of black sea-otter skin, fastened over one shoulder and leaving his arms free; at his waist was a wide belt of woven bark, decorated with different colored figures. The final touches were a highly polished copper ornament dangling from his nose, and several bracelets of copper and painted leather. Dressed for an important visit, Maquinna walked down to the water, followed by a group of his men, and got into his best ceremonial canoe. Standing in the stern, while his paddlers' powerful strokes made the craft glide swiftly and silently, he took off after the white men's ship.

The *Boston* was at anchor, and when the canoe came

alongside, Maquinna and his men went aboard. The chief, who had learned a little English from other traders, welcomed the ship's captain and officers to his country. In return, Captain Salter invited him to his cabin and offered him a glass of rum and some biscuits and molasses.

This was the first of several visits. In the meantime, the sailors were filling casks with fresh water, taking in wood, refitting the rigging, and fixing the sails. Many people from Maquinna's tribe brought fresh salmon, receiving in exchange a variety of objects, from scraps of metal to buttons. Captain Salter had heard of several attacks on ships by Indians of this coast, and to make sure that none came aboard armed, each was required to throw off his garment—except the chiefs. A group of these, together with their head chief Maquinna, had dinner with the captain, but ate only bread dipped in molasses, since they disliked the taste of salt which they never used. A few days later, Maquinna again was invited to dinner, and during his long talk with the captain, told him that near Friendly Cove there were many wild ducks and geese. Hearing this, Captain Salter presented a double-barreled hunting gun to the chief, who was much pleased with it.

Two days later, Maquinna visited the ship again, bringing eighteen ducks as a gift. He had the hunting gun with him, and was rather upset because one of it locks had broken. The gun was no good, he told the captain. Irked by Maquinna's remark, which he took as a personal insult, Salter called the chief a liar and went on with more offensive remarks. Then, grabbing the gun, he asked the ship's armorer to fix it. Maquinna, visibly hard put to restrain himself, said nothing, and soon after left with his men.

Maquinna had had unpleasant encounters with white men before. It was exactly twenty-five years since the famous Captain Cook, in March of 1778, had explored the coast of the Pacific Northwest and traded trinkets for sea-otter skins, later sold at fabulous prices in Chinese ports. Since then, many traders had visited Maquinna's country. In 1788, the Englishman John Meares had purchased from him for some copper and a pair of pistols a plot of land—soon taken over by Spaniards—and a dozen years later the American John Kendrick also bought some land on Nootka Sound. The British, Russians, Spaniards, and Americans were all intensely interested in the fur-rich Northwest; for several decades, its fate was uncertain—and nearly touched off a war in Europe —as different nations jockeyed for its control from nearby bases. Spain held California, which became part of the United States only in 1845. Russia owned Alaska and did not sell it to the U.S. government until 1867. England was firmly entrenched in Canada. The United States, still an Atlantic coast power, was about to purchase the immense Louisiana Territory from Napoleon, and thereby double size. And that same year, 1803, the explorers Lewis and Clark started on their transcontinental exploration to the West Coast.

Maquinna knew little of these great nations thousands of miles away. He was the head chief of one of several tribes, called Nootkas by the whites, who lived on Vancouver Island and on the northwestern tip of what is today the state of Washington. He was a powerful chief, and several tribes paid him tribute. But he lived much as his ancestors had lived— fishing and whaling, warring from time to time with his neighbors, feasting and holding elaborate religious ceremonies in which beautifully carved and painted masks and figures played an important part. At first, the arrival of big ships full of strange white men had little effect on the Nootkas' life. They brought iron, always scarce and always in demand to make chisels for wood carving. They brought rum and such delicacies as molasses. They brought beads and buttons and copper and other delightful objects of ornament. Maquinna and his people appreciated all these, and were willing to trade for them the otter skins that the white men seemed so anxious to get. But the coming of a ship didn't always mean peaceful trade. And on that spring day of 1803, as Maquinna left the *Boston* smarting under Captain Salter's insults, he remembered some of the events of the past quarter century.

He remembered the twenty Nootka warriors killed by Englishmen from one of the very first ships that moored at Friendly Cove. And the chiefs slaughtered by Spaniards who for awhile had a fort overlooking Friendly Cove. And the raid on Maquinna's own house—while the chief and his men were away—by the crew of a ship which had been welcomed by the Indians and had wintered in Nootka Sound. Maquinna remembered Callicum, a chief next to him in rank, who had been murdered by a Spanish officer and thrown overboard—and whose body could be recovered by his father only after payment of several otter skins. Now it was the white men's turn, thought Maquinna. The ship's people would have to pay for the wrongs suffered by the Nootkas. The chief called a council, that night, and laid careful plans.

The next morning, Indians visited the *Boston* as usual, bringing salmon, and stayed aboard. More of them followed a little later—always leaving their garments in the canoes to show they were not armed—accompanying Maquinna and several of his chiefs. Maquinna appeared to have forgotten the unpleasant episode of the day before; he had with him a wooden mask carved and painted to represent a fantastic beast, and once on board he put it on and began blowing on a whistle. His people started a grotesque dance, with many comic tricks which amused officers and crew. As the merrymaking went on, Maquinna talked with the captain, who told him that the ship would leave the morrow. "You love salmon," the chief suggested, "much in Friendly Cove, why not go there and catch some?" It seemed like a good idea, and ten men took off to go fishing, leaving only the captain and a dozen or so sailors aboard the *Boston* with Maquinna and his men.

All was going according to plans, and when the chief gave the signal, the Indians fell at once on the unsuspecting crew. Surprise and numbers made up for their lack of weapons, and soon they were masters of the ship. Arming themselves, they started after the fishing party, and easily dispatched the ten sailors. A row of severed heads, according to Northwest Indian custom, made bloody trophies for the victorious Nootkas.

Two of the *Boston* crew escaped the massacre. One was twenty-year-old John Jewitt, the ship's armorer, who had been busy at his workbench cleaning muskets, and was spared by Maquinna on condition that he become the chief's slave and work for him as gunsmith and blacksmith. The other survivor was sailmaker Thompson, a man of about forty, who had been hiding in the hold and was discovered only later. Jewitt passed him off as his father, and by playing on Maquinna's family feelings succeeded in saving his life. Both men were kept as slaves in the chief's household for nearly two and a half years.

Maquinna's house, which sheltered several families of relatives as well, was the largest in the village. It was a rectangular structure 40 feet wide, 150 feet long, and 14 feet high to the ridge of the gabled roof. A carved totem pole at the entrance symbolized the chief's high rank and achievements. Massive posts, carved in the shape of huge human heads, supported the ridgepole that was decorated with red and black bands. Other big timbers completed the sturdy post and beam framework, covered with heavy wood planks to form a roof and walls. These planks could be taken out. When the Nootkas moved to their winter quarters, they piled them in canoes and then placed them on the frameworks left standing in the winter village.

A wide passage ran through the middle, the whole length of the building, and on either side of the passage—without any dividing walls—were the quarters of the families that lived in it. Each family had a fireplace, built with rocks; in place of a chimney, a roof plank was lifted, by means of a pole, to let out the smoke. The simple furnishings included pine boxes for storing clothes, jewelry, and other valuable possessions, big wooden tubs for keeping blubber, the whale fat that was a staple in the Nootka's diet, and salmon spawn, the fish's caviarlike mass of eggs, and baskets for dried fish and other storage. Bark mats spread out on the dirt floor served as beds. Food was eaten from a hollowed-out tray. Half-a-dozen people would sit on the ground around it, their feet curled under them, and help themselves with their fingers or with clam shells. Maquinna and the other chiefs were the only people who had individual trays.

To celebrate his successful capture of the *Boston*, Maquinna held a potlatch, a mammoth feast to which people from a dozen or more tribes were invited. There were Kyuquots and Muchalats and Ahousats and Klayoquots— all Vancouver Island neighbors—as well as Indians from farther south, even from Cape Flattery on the Olympic Peninsula, who had traveled in their canoes well over a day up the coast to Nootka Sound. The language used by Indians at such intertribal gatherings was the Chinook jargon, which the Chinooks living at the mouth of the Columbia River had developed in their far-flung trade dealings with other tribes up and down the West Coast.

Maquinna gave his guests an elaborate welcome. His men, dressed up in assorted garments from the ship's cargo, squatted on the beach, holding the butts of their muskets down on the sand and waiting for an order to give a welcoming salute. In front of the village, a cannon from the ship had been mounted on heavy timbers, and was manned by Maquinna's new slave, sailmaker Thompson. The chief himself had climbed to the roof of his house, with a kind of wooden megaphone in hand, and from there gave the order to fire. The muskets went off and then the cannon. The Indians, acting as if they had been shot, rolled and tumbled on the beach—then suddenly got up and went into a frienzied victory song and dance. The ceremonies of welcome over, Maquinna led the guests to his house, where they were served a huge meal followed by an elaborate dance, to the accompaniment of a whistled tune, rattles, and drums.

The high point of the potlatch was the giving of gifts. Arranged in order of their rank, the guests were presented with cloth, muskets, casks of powder, looking glasses, and other items. As Maquinna proudly handed these out—in the name of his son and heir, Satsatsoksis—each recipient would snatch it from his hands with a sullen, almost hostile look, and the words, "Wocash, Tyee," meaning something like, "Hail, Chief." Each gesture, each expression followed ancient custom, and as often was the case with Northwest Indians, this potlatch lasted several days. Such important ceremonial feasts might be given for any number of reasons—to honor a dead chief, or announce the choice of an heir—and established the host's wealth and importance as a chief. The lavishness of the gift each guest received was commensurate with his rank, and the guests of highest standing would be expected in turn to give potlatches, presenting to the former host gifts of equal or sometimes even greater value.

Maquinna's pride in the rich booty he had gotten from the *Boston* was typical of the Northwest Indian's reverent attitude toward material possessions. And none of these—

Indians attending a potlatch wore their most elaborate robes and headdresses

house, jewelry, furs, canoes, weapons—rated higher than slaves. Maquinna had nearly fifty of them, both men and women, some taken in war and some bought from other tribes. They lived in his house and ate the same food as everyone else, but they were expected to work hard: cutting wood and fetching water, washing, building houses and canoes, fishing. And they never knew when, at a potlatch, their master might have one or more of them killed to prove to the assembled guests his great wealth.

The desire for slaves and booty, as well as disputes over fishing grounds or a good village site, often brought about war. The Nootkas fought not to win glory on the battlefield, but simply to win. The ideal, therefore, was to surprise the enemies in their sleep and bash their heads in before they could defend themselves. For just this purpose, Maquinna had his slave and blacksmith Jewitt fashion a special weapon: a sharp, six inch spike fastened at right angles to a longer iron handle, with a heavy knob as a joint fashioned into a man's head, whose eyes were made from black beads set in red sealing wax.

The chief was planning an expedition against the Echachets, who had left their winter quarters on Clayoquot Sound and were at their summer salmon-fishing village. The war preparations lasted three or four weeks. Several times a day, the warriors went to bathe and scrub themselves with prickly bushes, hard enough to draw blood—this was supposed to harden the skin so that weapons would not pierce it. During the last week, men went about with a thoughtful, almost gloomy expression, and refrained from feasting, games, or any kind of merrymaking. Finally, the appointed day came, and forty canoes took off, each carrying ten to twenty warriors. They took along no firearms, only daggers and war clubs, and some powerful short bows with whale-sinew strings, and three-foot-long arrows tipped with bone, copper, or a sharp piece of mussel shell.

The Echachet village was on a steep bank overlooking the river, and the canoes reached it about midnight. Maquinna decided to wait a few hours, so that the enemies would be surprised in their soundest sleep. The warriors landed silently and circled around to attack the village from the rear. When the first light of dawn broke the still summer night, they crept into the houses through the low door in the totem pole facing the entrance to each house. Maquinna had picked the house of the chief, and when he found him among the sleeping bodies, he gave him a fatal blow to the head. A triumphant war whoop was the signal to begin. Very few escaped. Still groggy with sleep, the villagers were either slaughtered or taken prisoners. The houses were destroyed. Loading the canoes with booty and with the newly acquired slaves, Maquinna and his warriors started back. Women and children received them with shouts of joy, and began drumming loudly on the house planks to accompany the men's victory song.

In addition to his roles as war leader, gift giver at potlatches, and main chief of the tribe, Maquinna was also the head harpooner. Only the few people who inherited his privilege were allowed to use a harpoon, and none could strike a whale until Maquinna had first drawn blood. The harpoon's line, some 350 feet long, had regularly spaced sealskin floats which slowed down the whale's flight. For the Nootkas whaling was nearly as exciting and dangerous as war, and required similar painstaking preparations on the men's part. In addition, Maquinna observed a strict ritual, including long solitary sessions of songs and prayers, designed to insure good luck. When successful, a whaling expedition was a boon to the Indians, for the huge beast provided not only a great quantity of meat, blubber, and oil, but also such materials as sinews and bones which could be used in dozens of ways.

With an ample supply of fish ready at hand, an occasional whale or some venison, and a wide variety of berries growing in the countryside, food was never much of a problem for the Nootkas and other Northwest Indians. Wood provided shelter, furnishings, clothing made of bark, and an easily worked material for all kinds of uses. Slaves often carried the burden of the heaviest jobs. Life was thus relatively rich and leisurely, and the Indians devoted much time to fashioning beautiful objects, developing imaginative religious ceremonies, and to colorful social activities. For a time, the traders, with their shiploads of goods, actually helped the Indians to enrich their lives and move toward an even more magnificent—if in many ways barbaric—culture. But the end was near.

In summer of 1805, Captain Hill anchored the *Lydia* of New York in Friendly Cove. Maquinna was tricked into releasing Jewitt and Thompson, but far from being resentful he promised the trader that he would have a load of skins on the ship's next call there. The *Lydia* sailed down the coast, and at the mouth of the Columbia River, Indians came aboard wearing medals with a picture of President Jefferson on them. They had received them, they said, from two captains called Lewis and Clark. The United States had successfully completed a major transcontinental exploration, and soon the West Coast could be reached more easily by land than by the long hazardous sea route around Cape Horn. Covered wagons would cross the plains, and settlers would start moving in—first into California, then into Oregon and Washington. Maquinna's world survived only a few more decades. There was just enough time for a last splendid burst of artistic creation—sculpture and colorful garments and beautifully carved and painted masks.

8

Tecumseh's Great Dream
of Indian Unity

◦⁓⁓◦

THE STREETS of Vincennes, capital of the Indian territory, were filled with American soldiers, and several cavalry and infantry units stood ready to swing into action. In his mansion, Indiana's governor, William Henry Harrison, was waiting. A sword at his side, he was surrounded by the town's most distinguished citizens and Indiana's top officials; an honor guard—pistols in their belts—stood nearby.

Tecumseh was on his way for a council, and in that summer of 1810, the prospect of a visit from the powerful chief was enough to make any U.S. official in frontier country understandably worried.

Strong and slim, his straight figure dressed in plain buckskin, Tecumseh wore a single eagle feather in the handkerchief covering his hair. With him went thirty young Shawnee warriors. Decked in brilliant red paint, they had no weapons but their tomahawks, thrust into the belts of their neatly fitted deerskin breeches.

For the third time in nine days, there would be a council on the grounds of the governor's mansion. The two protagonists were impressive men. Tecumseh, the chief from a Shawnee tribe, had already become a legend around the campfires for his bravery and cunning in battle, and for his forceful eloquence. Governor Harrison, the gentleman from Virginia, had distinguished himself as an aide to General Wayne in his successful campaign against the Indians of the Ohio, and would later be elected President of the United States. The issue before them was that of a hundred earlier councils: land, and the relations between settlers and Indians. But this time there was something new—Tecumseh was not speaking for the rights of one tribe, or even for an alliance of tribes. He was speaking for all Indians.

He told Governor Harrison,

> Once they were a happy race. Now they are made miserable by the white people who are never contented but forever encroaching. The way, the only way, to check and stop this evil is for all the red men to unite in claiming a common and equal right to the land. That is how it was at first, and should be still, for the land never was divided but belongs to all, for the use of everyone. No groups among us have a right to sell, even to one another, much less to strangers who want all and will not do with less. . . . Sell a country! Why not sell the air, the clouds, and the great sea, as well as the earth?

The United States, Tecumseh pointed out, "set the example of forming a union among all the fires—why should they censure the Indians for following it?"

At the end of the chief's impassioned speech, the governor sat silent for a few minutes, then rose to reply. But he had just begun to speak when—as he was stating that the United States had dealt quite fairly with the Indians—he was vehemently interrupted by Tecumseh. "It is false! He lies!" the chief shouted, and went on to denounce Harrison in the strongest language. The governor drew his sword, several men grabbed their pistols, a dozen riflemen rushed up. The thirty warriors, tomahawks in hand, closed behind

Violence threatened to disrupt the council between Tecumseh and Governor Harrison

Tecumseh ready for action. But the tense confrontation didn't break out into a fight. The governor, brusquely adjourning the council, retired to the mansion, and the angry Shawnees stalked away.

The next day, tempers had cooled off. Harrison visited Tecumseh at his camp, and while they sat together on a bench discussing U.S.–Indian land treaties, the chief began shifting his position and crowding the governor. When Harrison found himself at the end of the bench, he complained. Tecumseh's reply was a laugh. Obviously it was not pleasant, he remarked, to find oneself constantly crowded out of places—that's what kept happening to the Indians.

The meetings between Harrison and Tecumseh failed to

produce agreement. Harrison was committed to getting from the Indians "sufficient space to form a tolerable state." As he told the Indiana legislature: "Is one of the finest portions of the globe to remain in a state of nature, the haunt of a few wretched savages, when it seems destined, by the Creator, to give support to a large population, and to be the seat of civilization, of science, and true religion?"

Harrison shared the average frontiersman's view of the Indians as "wretched savages," but his opinion of Tecumseh was very high. In a report to Washington, he later wrote that Tecumseh was an "uncommon genius" and added that "if it were not for the vicinity of the United States, he would perhaps be the founder of an Empire that would rival in glory that of Mexico or Peru."

Tecumseh's road to a position of leadership and prestige that no other Indian chief ever attained, was not easy. Born a few years after the end of Pontiac's war, in a Shawnee village not far from present-day Dayton, Tecumseh saw clashes between Indians and settlers from his earliest childhood. He was not quite seven when one evening he and his mother went out to look for his father, who had not returned home. They found him dying, shot in the breast by one of a band of frontiersmen.

From that day on, a deep hatred for the white men filled Tecumseh's heart, and he longed to fight them and avenge his father's death. The total destruction of his native Shawnee town by an American army during the Revolutionary War, kindled his hatred, and in his early teens he became a fighter. He had always shown great prowess in hunting and sports, but at his first battle he lost his nerve. When the gunfire began, blind fear gripped him and drove him to sudden flight. That evening, by the campfire, as the brave warriors were commended, there was no word for Tecumseh. He was not censured. The Shawnees seldom reprimanded or gave orders to their young. They were taught by example and commendation, and left to be the judges of their own shortcomings. Tecumseh could have found no sterner judge than his own heart, and would never again show fear or be anything but last to leave the battle.

At the end of the Revolutionary War, the British withdrew to Canada, and more settlers began crossing the Ohio River and taking over Indian land. Shawnee war parties fought them at every turn. After one encounter in which Tecumseh took part, the warriors tied a captured settler to a stake and burned him. Fifteen-year-old Tecumseh watched with growing horror, and finally, leaping to his feet, lashed out with fiery words at the indignity of this torture. It was not worthy of warriors, but of the lowest beast! He, Tecumseh, would not allow it ever to happen again before him. For all his hatred of the white men and his fierce courage in battle, young Tecumseh had already acquired the compassion and the contempt for cruelty that marked him throughout life. Again and again, white prisoners were to report with gratitude and admiration his generosity and his firmness in restraining other warriors bent on bloody massacres.

Border warfare raged on. Tecumseh became chief of a band of young warriors and took part in victorious actions against General Harmar and later against General St. Clair, who lost one-third of his two thousand men in one of the worst defeats the American army ever suffered. In 1792, the twenty-four-year-old chief went south to join one of his older brothers who was helping the Cherokees and Creeks fight Tennessee settlers. Tecumseh's brother was killed during an attack on a fort near Nashville, and soon after the chief and his band returned to the Ohio country. Another Shawnee leader, Chief Blue Jacket, needed help against a new powerful army under General Wayne. The decisive battle was the Battle of Fallen Timbers, so called because its site was strewn with big trees, blown down by a tornado.

Blue Jacket had ranged his warriors behind the fallen

trees, in a strong position. But they faced more than twice as many soldiers, trained in range firing and bayonet charge, supported by artillery and well-mounted dragoons. Even though chiefs and braves fought valiantly, they suffered a disastrous defeat. Tecumseh and his band held their ground to the very last. When most of the other Indians had fled, they charged, scattering a group of soldiers manning a fieldpiece and taking their horses.

General Wayne followed up his victory with the destruction of village after village, forcing the vanquished Indians to agree in 1795 to the Greenville Treaty. The United States acquired by this treaty nearly two-thirds of Ohio and a wedge of Indiana. Most of the chiefs who had led the fighting signed the treaty, and from then on respected its terms. A Shawnee's commitment to his word was so strong that if one individual didn't honor a debt, the tribe would collect the amount needed and pay in full.

Tecumseh condemned the Greenville Treaty, and refused to sign it. With a band of followers he moved west to Indiana, and from then on he was looked upon as *the* chief, the one leader who refused to submit and might in time march at the head of the Shawnees and other tribes—to rescue for the Indians their beautiful country of the Ohio.

During this period of relative peace, Tecumseh came to know settler James Galloway and his family, and fell in love with the pretty, blond Rebecca Galloway. Intelligent and educated, she took on the task of teaching him. She read to him books from her father's three hundred volume library—a remarkable one in pioneer country. She read from the Bible and Shakespeare and history books—later Tecumseh would talk about Alexander the Great. She helped Tecumseh improve his English, and under her influence his natural compassion matured into a profoundly humane attitude toward life.

Tecumseh wanted to marry Rebecca, his "Star of the Lake." When he asked for her hand, her father was not adverse, and the girl accepted—but on one condition. He must take up the way of life of her community, and turn his back on Indian customs, dress, and manner of living. For a month, Tecumseh debated with himself, but there was really no choice. He could not become a white man, he could not leave his people. He saw Rebecca one last time, to tell her his answer, and then left her forever.

In councils and around the campfires, Tecumseh was becoming known as the best spokesman for the Indians' rights. Whenever he addressed an audience, his wise and passionate words swung more people toward his views. And now his younger brother, Laulewasika, added to Tecumseh's leadership the fervor of a religious crusade. Long considered a lazy, good-for-nothing drunkard, Laulewasika had been converted suddenly to a set of religious principles demanding complete abstinence from liquor and a return to the ancient way of life. Known now as the Prophet, he teamed with Tecumseh in rallying the Indians against the settlers, and his teachings spread from Ohio and Indiana, north and west to and beyond the Mississippi.

Indiana's governor, William Henry Harrison, followed the rising influence of the Prophet among many tribes with an anxious eye. Trying to discredit him, Harrison suggested that he give proof of his spiritual authority by performing a miracle. The Prophet took up the challenge. On June 16, he said, he would make the sun darken. On that day a huge crowd assembled to witness the miracle, and standing in its middle the Prophet waited. He was dressed in a flowing garment as dark as the raven's wings that crowned his head. Everyone watched the clear sky. At 11:32 A.M., the Prophet raised his hand, just as the moon began covering the sun. Filled with awe and fear, the crowd heard him call out to the Master of

Life to lift his hand from the sun's face—and light returned. Thus, by the masterly exploitation of an eclipse, the Prophet turned the tables on Harrison, and from then on tales of his miracles spread far and wide on the prairie.

Meanwhile, Tecumseh was engaged in finding converts to his cause, traveling from tribe to tribe and laying the foundations of a great alliance. Indian unity might, when the proper time came, defeat the Long Knives—as the saber-carrying Americans were called—and establish a free, independent Indian nation. From Lake Superior to the Gulf of Mexico, from the Ohio River to the Missouri, the fiery message of Tecumseh was spreading unrest and inspiring young warriors to side with him against the advice of their old chiefs who were urging caution and friendship with the Americans at all costs.

The last step that made war between the Indians and the expanding United States inevitable was taken by Governor Harrison in the fall of 1809. He gathered together a number of the weaker chiefs, and using promises, liquor, and $7,000 in cash he talked them into signing the Treaty of Fort Wayne. Some three million acres of land, the heart of present-day Indiana, were taken away from the Indians, including the hunting grounds of Tecumseh's tribe, none of whom were present at the negotiations.

The lines were drawn. Tecumseh knew that he must fight, but he was not ready. He had about a thousand warriors in the Prophet's town on the Tippecanoe River, and could count on many more. He was well aware, however, of the strength the United States could muster in an all-out war; he must have the support of more tribes and of the British forces in Canada, and for this he needed time. Harrison, on the other hand, was eager to break up the power of Tecumseh and his brother, the Prophet, so that there would be no organized opposition to the white settlement of Indiana.

When the great chief and the frontier governor met in Vincennes, each was thus determined to further his cause and yield nothing. The council could not have produced an agreement; it was merely a sparring rehearsal of the bloody duel to come. A few episodes of violence—from both whites and Indians—heightened the border tension in the spring of 1811. "I consider peace as totally out of the question. We need not expect it until the Prophet's party is dispersed," Harrison wrote in a report to the government in Washington.

Tecumseh set off on a six-month journey to enlist the support of more tribes. He went south to the Chickasaws, the Choctaws, the Creeks, the Seminoles, the Cherokees—and then west to the powerful Osages in Arkansas and Missouri, and to the Iowas. Again and again he spoke to chiefs and warriors gathered in solemn council.

> Where today are the Pequots? Where the Narragansetts, the Mohicans, the Pokanokets and many other once powerful tribes of our people? They have vanished before the rapaciousness and oppression of the white man, as snow before a summer sun. In the vain hope of defending alone their ancient possessions, they have fallen. . . . The destruction of our race is at hand, unless we unite in one common cause against the common foe.

Tecumseh's passionate call for union and the frenzied Shawnee war dance he and his two dozen young braves staged stirred the audience deeply. The Creeks and the Seminoles responded to the call and declared their readiness to fight the Long Knives. But among other tribes the cautious older chiefs succeeded in restraining the enthusiasm of the young warriors who wanted to join Tecumseh. Ancient enmities among tribes, the lack of present danger from settlers in some areas, the illusion that the tribe could best deal with the United States by itself—these and other reasons worked against Tecumseh. Discouraged by the scant progress he had

made toward his dream of Indian union, the chief started
home. And when he reached the Tippecanoe River, he
found the Prophet's town in ashes.

Governor Harrison had decided to take advantage of Tecumseh's absence to march against the Prophet. The United
States government had no part in this decision. In fact, President James Madison did not want a border war with the Indians, since it might lead to a conflict with the British in
Canada. Instructions received by Harrison from the Secretary
of War stressed Madison's "earnest desire that peace may, if
possible, be preserved with the Indians, and that to this end
every proper means be adopted." But Harrison was committed
to the settlers' aims: breaking up the Indians' power to get
more and more land. With an army of nearly a thousand men,
the governor marched toward the Tippecanoe.

In the Prophet's town no one expected war. Tecumseh had
ordered his brother to avoid fighting, but a band of Winne-
bagos argued that they could defeat Harrison, and it was
decided that the Indians would attack the American camp
that night. The battle began at four in the morning, when a
warrior was spotted and shot by a sentry; his comrades immediately charged with loud war whoops, alerting all the
soldiers. The plan to break suddenly through the center of
the camp and kill Harrison failed. The Indians tried several
more attacks, but they were outnumbered two-to-one. The
camp's position was strategically strong, and Harrison led his
men bravely. There was nothing left for the Prophet's forces
to do but retire.

Unopposed, Harrison marched into the Prophet's town
and destroyed everything in it—food, possessions, buildings.
The victory of Tippecanoe had cost him 61 dead and 127
wounded; only 30 or 40 Indians were dead. Yet in a report
to the Secretary of War in Washington Harrison wrote:
"The Indians have never sustained so severe a defeat since

The battle of Tippacanoe in 1871 aroused the Indians to war

their acquaintance with the white people." Growing more impressive as the years went by, this minor skirmish came to be considered a major battle. In 1840, its memory helped elect the Harrison-Tyler presidential ticket, to the refrain of "Tippecanoe and Tyler too."

The immediate result of Harrison's march on the Prophet's town was a wave of violence throughout Indiana and Illinois. Bands of warriors went on the warpath and attacked settlers without plan and without clear purpose except revenge. Tecumseh was enraged by Harrison's destruction of his town, but he was even angrier at his brother for having allowed the battle to take place, and the Prophet was stripped of all power. The Prophet lost most of his followers, and though he still preached his gospel of a return to the simple, ancient ways of life, he soon disappeared into obscurity. The damage, however, was already done, and the recurrent clashes on the frontier soon led to the war for which Tecumseh was not ready.

It broke out on June 18, 1812, when the United States declared war on Great Britain, who was believed to be inciting the Indians to violence. General William Hull, on his way to Detroit and an invasion of Canada, sent envoys to Tecumseh and other chiefs to secure their neutrality. But Tecumseh never hesitated.

He told a council,

> Here is a chance presented to us. Yes, a chance such as will never occur again—for us Indians of North America to form ourselves into one great combination and cast our lot with the British in this war. And should they conquer and again get the mastery of all North America, our rights to at least a portion of the land of our fathers would be respected by the King. If they should not win and the whole country should pass into the hands of the Long Knives—we see this plainly—it will not be many years before our last place of abode and our last hunting ground will be taken from us,

and the remnants of the different tribes between the Mississippi, the Lakes, and the Ohio River will all be driven toward the setting sun.

In early July, Tecumseh was at Fort Malden in Canada, downstream and across the river from Detroit. The British had a garrison of three hundred; General Hull had three thousand men—with artillery and cavalry—and crossing the Detroit River he marched toward Fort Malden. The defense of western Canada was in the hands of Tecumseh and his warriors. A few skirmishes and ambushes checked the advance of the wary General Hull. A surprise attack on his supply line inflicted heavy casualties; even more important, it led to the capture of the general's dispatches and of soldiers' letters—which were to show the British how weak Hull's leadership was and how much his men mistrusted him. Worried by his losses, General Hull next heard that Chippewas and Ottawas had helped the British capture Michilimackinack Island, and might be canoeing down Lake Huron to attack him. Giving up all invasion plans, Hull retreated hastily to Detroit.

The British now took the initiative. General Isaac Brock had just reached Fort Malden with three hundred additional troops. A tall, powerful man who combined iron determination with imagination and a suprisingly gentle nature, Brock held a council with his staff and the Indian chiefs the night he arrived. Against the advice of all but one of his officers, he decided in favor of Tecumseh's plan to attack Detroit immediately. Twelve hours later, the British and the Indians were on the march.

Move followed move in rapid succession. Tecumseh and six hundred warriors crossed the Detroit River, and in the darkness surrounded the town and fort. Across the river, Brock installed a battery trained on the fort. A British courier was allowed conveniently to fall into Hull's hands, so that the already worried general could read a dispatch about five thousand Indians supposedly rushing down from Michilimackinack. Finally, Brock and his troops crossed the river, ready to attack.

While the British battery kept shelling the fort, Brock and Tecumseh inspected their lines on horseback. The chief wore deerskin leggings, breechcloth, and moccasins; his face and body were streaked with war paint; a single eagle's feather was in his black hair. Riding next to him on a grey charger was General Brock in a splendid scarlet and gold uniform, shining boots, and cocked hat. Brock had quickly appraised the Indian's keen mind, his sure grasp of strategy, his gift for leadership. Without him, the British would have been lost. Brock's judgment was confirmed a few moments later. Tecumseh had his warriors march out of the woods and through a clearing—three times over—so that Hull would think thousands of Indians had arrived from the north. It worked. As Brock was about to order the attack, a white flag fluttered over Fort Detroit.

The stunning victory shocked the frontier settlements and drew more tribes into the war against the Long Knives. It gave Tecumseh real hope that the United States might be forced to give up claim to the land between the Ohio, the Great Lakes, and the Mississippi. An independent Indian country seemed no longer a dream. But to make it come true the Indians must not only win on the battlefield, they must also earn the white men's respect. Statesmanship as well as Tecumseh's humane outlook made him acutely aware of how important his warriors' good behavior was to his cause. He allowed no violence or plundering in the captured town of Detroit, and throughout the campaign he strove to keep his warriors from harming settlers or prisoners.

On one occasion, he needed meat to feed his men, and took two oxen from a boy working in a field. When the boy

Prisoners were protected from harm by Tecumseh's firm discipline of his warriors

complained that his family was poor and couldn't make a living without the oxen, Tecumseh replied: "We are the conquerors and everything we want is ours. I must have the oxen, but I will not be so mean as to rob you of them. I will pay you $100 for them, and that is more than they are worth." He then sent the boy to the British Indian agent to collect the money. Later, the boy came back saying the agent had refused to pay. Tecumseh immediately went back with him, had him paid in full, and added an extra dollar. "Take that," he said. "It will pay you for the time you have lost in getting your money."

A month after the capture of Detroit, Tecumseh and thirty of his best warriors started on a long journey south.

The year before, the Creeks had responded to his appeal for unity. Now he might get them to strike at the Long Knives, helped by the Seminoles and supplied with arms, ammunition, and food by British ships in the Gulf of Mexico. News of Indian victories in the Great Lakes region had already stirred unrest, and Tecumseh's fiery words found ready listeners. The Creek Confederation soon after went on the warpath. The resulting conflict claimed thousands of lives throughout the South, and cost the United States millions of dollars. The Creeks were eventually crushed by Andrew Jackson, whose brilliant military leadership gained him national reputation and later helped him win election as President of the United States.

While Tecumseh was in the South, the brave and imaginative General Brock had been killed in battle. His successor as British commander was General Procter, who looked down on the Indians and had none of the qualities of bold leadership common to both Brock and Tecumseh. The warriors returned Procter's contempt and paid no attention to his orders. After a smashing victory against a division of 850 Kentuckians, a group of Indians butchered nearly all of the wounded prisoners. This massacre at River Raisin, which Procter did not prevent, enraged the Americans and spurred their war effort.

Tecumseh brought back with him another six hundred men, and had under him a powerful army of nearly three thousand warriors. Procter had one thousand soldiers. Facing them now was General Harrison, and Tecumseh looked forward with pleasure to the opportunity of avenging Harrison's destruction of the Prophet's town. The Indians and British surrounded Fort Meigs, where Harrison was encamped, and inflicted a bloody defeat on a brigade of reinforcements—480 were killed and 150 taken prisoners. While these were taken to Procter's headquarters, the Indians killed several of them; and even after the captives were inside the stockade, under a British guard, warriors came after their scalps. Procter made no move to stop the massacre, but word of what was happening reached Tecumseh. In a rage, the chief raced over and lunged at the Indians with a shout: "Are there no men here?" His fury cowed the bloodthirsty warriors, and as they slunk away Tecumseh looked for Procter. Calling him a squaw, the chief reproached the general for allowing such murders. "You are unfit to command," he said.

Relations between the two men, who had never liked each other, grew worse as time went on. Tecumseh considered Procter a coward who would not seize the opportunity to wage a vigorous campaign. After Commodore Perry defeated the British fleet on Lake Erie, Procter not only gave up any thought of attacking, but prepared to retreat. Afraid of what the Indians might do, the general said nothing of his plans. But Tecumseh understood, and once again upbraided him:

> We are sorry to see that you are getting ready to flee before you ever have sight of the enemy—like a fat animal that carries its tail on its back, but, when frightened, drops it between its legs and runs. . . . You have the arms and ammunition which our great father sent for his red children. If you have any idea of going away, give them to us, and you may go and welcome. Our lives are in the hands of the Great Spirit. He gave to our ancestors the lands which we possess. We are determined to defend them, and if it is His will, our bones shall whiten on them, but we will never give them up.

Procter, however, was determined to seek safety with the rest of the British army in eastern Canada. Only his fear of the Indians wrung from him a promise that he would make a stand at the Thames River. As Tecumseh reluctantly followed the British eastward, Harrison's army—3500 men strong—was in pursuit. Several quarrels with Procter could not make him heed Tecumseh's advice and take the initiative when the occasion for attack presented itself. At the crossing of the Thames, the chief decided to hold ground even though the British had already further withdrawn. The Indians fought Harrison's vanguard valiantly, but after thirteen of them had been killed and many others wounded, Tecumseh decided to rejoin the British. He had been shot in the arm, but bandaged it and continued fighting.

That evening, Tecumseh attempted once more to get Procter to act, proposing a bold plan for a night attack on Harrison. They had seven hundred soldiers and some one thousand warriors. Surprise and the cover of darkness might offset Harrison's advantage of twice that many men. Procter refused. Later that night, Tecumseh and his closest followers gathered around the campfire. A group of Wyandots had gone over to the American side—another blow to the cause that now seemed almost lost. The chief was silent awhile, then quietly began to speak: "Brother warriors, we are about to enter an engagement from which I shall not return. My body will remain on the field of battle."

The morning of October 5, 1813, Harrison's main force crossed the Thames and began marching upstream along its northern bank. Tecumseh faced Procter, rifle in hand, and forced him to agree to give battle. But it was the chief, not the general, who took charge. He placed the British soldiers across the road on which the Americans would march. It was a strong position: the deep, swift Thames covered the left flank, and a wooded swamp the right. His own warriors were in formation beyond this swamp, extending forward and to the right so as to command the road. Waiting for Harrison, Tecumseh inspected the lines, shaking hands with the British officers and finding for all warm words of encouragement.

Loud and clear from up the road came the sound of bugles, and then 1500 Kentucky horsemen charged, shooting their rifles and yelling, "Remember the River Raisin!" The first British line collapsed, and as the Kentuckians smashed through their ranks, General Procter, who had been safely in the rear, rushed into his carriage and sped away. Caught between the cavalry, now at their back, and Harrison's infantry, the British surrendered.

The Kentuckians' charge against Tecumseh's position, however, had been stopped by heavy, steady fire. Dismounting, they began fighting the Indians at the edge of the woods. Tecumseh seemed to be everywhere at once, his bold voice spurring on his warriors. Wounded again and again, his clothes smeared with blood, the great chief fought on, still shouting to his men to stand firm and throw back the attackers. The Indians ran out of ammunition and were fighting with their tomahawks, slowly yielding ground. Darkness fell, and with it the great stillness that follows battle. The Americans encamped near the river, guarding nearly six hundred British prisoners they had taken—no Indians had been captured.

The warriors who survived fled through the wooded swamps, but Tecumseh was not with them. As he had foreseen the night before, his body remained on the field of battle, and the small group of followers who had sat around the campfire with him came back during the night to secretly bury their great chief. For years to come, white men wondered whether Tecumseh might still be alive, and legends grew around his mysterious end.

Harrison's victory at the Battle of the Thames and Tecumseh's death sealed the fate of the Indians of the Ohio country and opened to the settlers the gateway to the Great Plains. There would be more struggles, other tribes would rise under brave leaders to fight the invaders. But the great dream of an independent Indian nation died forever with Tecumseh. At the Treaty of Ghent negotiations, which in 1814 closed the war between England and the United States, the British at-

The Indians were defeated and Tecumseh was killed at the Battle of the Thames

tempted to create an Indian state that would act as a buffer between Canada and the United States. But the Americans, who had fought to gain control of the territory, were not about to give it up. British insistence gave way before the desire for re-establishing the peace, and the strong Indian voice that might have demanded better terms for his people was now stilled. As Tecumseh had predicted, the Indians were pushed beyond the Mississippi. Plowed land and the bustle of cities took the place of the deep woods. And the march westward of the now more powerful new nation continued across the continent.

9

Sequoyah the Cherokee: The Magic of Learning

IT WAS A council such as no Indian tribe had ever held. The leading men of the Cherokee nation had gathered not to decide on peace or war, not to choose a chief, not to debate the move to new hunting grounds—but to judge the invention of a fellow tribesman. For twelve years Sequoyah had been at work on it. He had been laughed at by some, who thought his efforts were a silly waste of time. He had been called a sorcerer by others, who felt he was dabbling in forbidden magic. Now Sequoyah's great day had come. He could show the people of his tribe the result of his long labors—and he knew that its importance went far beyond any choice ever made of hunting grounds, a new chief, or even peace or war.

Sequoyah took his place at one spot, with one of his children some distance away at another. Then, as a huge crowd looked on, the test began. Someone gave Sequoyah a sentence, and he made a few marks on a piece of paper; a trusted messenger took it to Sequoyah's child, who looked at it and repeated the message word by word. Again and again, Sequoyah's "talking leaves" spoke in Cherokee, and gradually the spectators' awe and admiration found expression in enthusiastic cheers. To the Cherokees, for whom writing had been until then white man's magic, this was an incredible achievement.

Like the other Indian languages of North America, Cherokee had been spoken for centuries, but never written. White
missionaries who had tried to write it down had decided that
no combinations of English vowels and consonants could
adequately reproduce its sounds. It took the genius of Sequoyah to give the Cherokees the gift of writing. A man
who had gone to no school and didn't even know, when he
started, what writing was. He had heard that white men
could send one another "talking leaves," but apparently had
not had an opportunity to become acquainted with one of
these until after he had already begun working on an alphabet, when he chanced to find a piece of a newspaper.

Sequoyah was born in the village of Tuskegee, near the
Tennessee River, a few years before the American Revolution. The Cherokees, once the most powerful of the southeastern tribes, still held several million acres of land in
northern Georgia, Alabama, and Tennessee. In 1791, the
United States had guaranteed the Cherokees' rights to this
country in a solemn treaty. Renouncing force as a means to
further its welfare, the tribe began to progress toward a civilized society patterned after that of the new American nation. Sturdy buildings with log walls and shake roofs replaced
the earlier thatched houses. The Indians built roads and
schools, inviting missionaries to come and teach. After learning to use the white man's tools, they became farmers, took
up the loom and started stockbreeding. Many of them grew
prosperous. Some were wealthy enough to own Negro
slaves who worked their plantations, and to live as comfortably as any of their white neighbors. They had always had a
basically democratic form of government. Early in the
1800's they adopted formal laws, which were written in English, and later developed a constitution modeled after that of
the United States.

The period of peace enjoyed by most of the Cherokees
around 1800—a time relatively free from the westward push

of settlers—was ideal for the development of an imaginative young man like Sequoyah. Since early boyhood he had been fascinated by drawing—at first scratching crude figures on a tree with a hunting knife, then beginning to paint on pieces of bark or animal skin. Using charcoal, red ochre, and many colored dyes, which he prepared from berries and plant roots, Sequoyah painted animals, people, scenes of Indian life. His skill was remarkable, and according to one contemporary, "no man in the United States can surpass him in drawing a buffalo." From painting, Sequoyah went on to silversmithing, and on his crude forge he fashioned beautiful earrings, bracelets, spoons, and spurs much in demand among his fellow Indians.

One day, some young men were talking about the wonderful things white men could do, and one fellow mentioned that they could talk on a piece of paper and send it to another person far away who could understand what it said. That was easy, Sequoyah remarked, and picking up a flat stone he made some marks on it. Each mark represented a word, he explained, and thus could talk. The company laughed, and the subject was dropped. But the thought stayed with him, and from that time on—the year was 1809—he began looking for ways to make paper talk in Cherokee. First, he tried designing a symbol for each word; but soon he had several thousands of them, too many for everyone to learn and use. After months and years of experimenting with one method and another, he finally discovered that words could be divided into parts. These parts, or syllables, kept recurring in many words, so that with relatively few signs (each representing a syllable) he could put together any word.

From 1809 to 1821 Sequoyah worked on devising and perfecting his invention. Meanwhile, he had put aside his artistic pursuits for more practical labors. Instead of jewelry, he had been shaping farm tools on his forge—hoes, rakes, spades. They were superior in design and workmanship to those then available, and they were eagerly sought by Cherokees and settlers alike. Sequoyah stamped them with a die bearing his English name, George Guess. (While his mother was a full-blooded Indian, and he grew up and lived all his life among the Cherokees, his father was said to have been a Virginian, variously identified as Guess, Guest, or Gist.)

As George Guess, Sequoyah served with the U.S. army in the War of 1812, although disabled in one leg since early youth. The Cherokees had temporarily found prosperity through peaceful agreements with the United States, and they did not heed Tecumseh's call for Indian union against the Long Knives. In fact, several hundred warriors—including Sequoyah—fought with General Jackson's army and helped him win a decisive victory over the Creeks at the Battle of Horseshoe Bend. The defeat of the British, and later of the Spaniards, eliminated both these foreign influences from the Southeast. Indian allies were no longer important to the United States, and the state of Georgia was eyeing the lands of the Cherokees. Many Indians, foreseeing what was to come, began to move west of the Mississippi.

In 1818, Sequoyah joined a party of 330 Cherokees migrating to Arkansas, where a colony of a thousand fellow tribesmen was already established. The emigrants started down the Tennessee River on a flotilla of flatboats loaded with their household goods and other possessions. Their leader, Chief Jolly, writing to authorities in Washington said, "You must not think that by removing we shall return to the savage life. You have learned us to be herdsmen and cultivators, and to spin and weave."

In his new home on the Arkansas River, Sequoyah continued working at his alphabet. By 1821, he had it perfected to the point where he could write down messages from the Cherokee emigrants to take back with him to their friends in the east. These messages aroused such interest and so dramatized the great usefulness of his invention, that the leaders

Cherokee Alphabet.

D o	R e	T i	δo	O u	i v
S ga O ka	F ge	y gi	A go	J gu	E gv
θha	P he	θhi	F ho	Γhu	Ωhv
W la	σle	P li	G lo	M lu	θlv
δma	O me	H mi	$5 mo$	y mu	
θna t hna G nah	Λne	h ni	Z no	θnu	O nv
T qua	ωque	P qui	V quo	ωquu	E quv
U sa ωs	4 se	b si	F so	E su	R sv
L da W ta	S de T te	J di J ti	V do	S du	θdv
δdla L tla	L tle	C tli	θtlo	θtlu	P tlv
G tsa	V tse	h tsi	K tso	J tsu	C tsv
G wa	ωwe	θwi	θwo	θwu	6 wv
ωya	B ye	δyi	h yo	G yu	B yv

Sequoyah developed the Cherokee Alphabet

of the Cherokee nation decided to call a council and put it to a thorough test. That solemn and most unusual council was convinced beyond doubt that Sequoyah had unlocked the secret of the "talking leaves." The Cherokees' response was immediate and incredibly enthusiastic. Within months, thousands of them had learned to read and write. Young braves took time off from hunting or working in the fields, women from their spinning wheels. Young or old, everybody seemed to share in the excitement of the new learning. Sequoyah, "the Master," soon became one of the most respected members of the tribe. In 1825, the General Council of the Cherokee Nation had a silver medal made to honor him "for his ingenuity in the invention of the Cherokee alphabet."

The settlers, hungry for land, were already beginning to gnaw at the Arkansas colony. White settlements were closing in on this part of the tribe, and they were subjected to harassment by cattle and horse thieves. In 1828, a western Cherokee delegation went to Washington in an attempt to iron out with the U.S. government some of these problems. Sequoyah was one of its members. The discussions in the capital resulted in a new treaty, by which the Cherokees of Arkansas once again agreed to move farther west, to what is now Sequoyah County in Oklahoma. Four of the delegation signed the treaty in Cherokee characters.

A few months before, the first Indian newspaper, the *Cherokee Phoenix*, printed partly in English and partly in Cherokee, was issued. This achievement heightened public interest in Sequoyah, and during his stay in Washington he was the center of much attention. The painter Charles Bird King asked him to sit for a portrait, and scholars and writers sought him out.

Back at his home on the Arkansas River, Sequoyah and his fellow tribesmen prepared to leave the thriving community they had established, and move again to a western wilderness. There were 2500 of them, but the migration took place without many difficulties or serious hardships. Much as they hated to leave their homes and farms, Sequoyah and the other leaders of the western Cherokees realized that they could not stop the expansion of the white frontier. War against the United States, with its superior strength both in numbers and equipment, could only end in bloody defeat. Better to withdraw and hope that eventually the swelling westward wave might subside and leave enough land for the Indians to live comfortably and in peace.

In Oklahoma, Sequoyah settled down to a simple life on the farm he cleared for himself in the wilderness. He tended his crops, raised some cattle, poultry, and hogs. He also had title to a salt lick that provided him with additional income; from time to time he would hitch his ox team to a cart, load it with supplies and tools, and travel the dozen miles to the salt lick. Here he would fill big kettles with water from the salt springs, put them over a fire which he fed until the water had evaporated—leaving salt at the bottom. Then he would scoop the salt up, and start all over, until he had enough for his customers.

But his own work never kept him from pursuing his vocation as teacher. Whenever a visitor would call on him, he would gladly explain how his alphabet worked, and from time to time he traveled through western Cherokee country, stopping to teach reading and writing to any who asked him. New arrivals from the east kept increasing the size of the colony, which over a decade grew to about five or six thousand people.

While the Cherokees in Oklahoma were peacefully establishing a new farming settlement, the main body of the tribe in Georgia was facing more serious problems. Gold had been found in their country, and gold fever, added to the demand for land, sealed their fate. In answer to the pressures of the frontier states, Congress in 1830 passed the Indian removal bill, authorizing the President to negotiate with tribes for the exchange of their present lands for others west of the Mississippi. The full weight of federal, state, and local government was brought to bear on the Indians to give up their lands. State laws stripped them of any rights, and by violence or fraud unscrupulous whites took over their property. As conditions grew worse, tribal leaders began accepting treaties of removal, and thousands of Choctaws, Chickasaws, and Creeks were herded away, often losing all their possessions and suffering incredible hardships.

The Cherokees appealed to Congress and the courts for protection of the rights granted them by government treaties. The Supreme Court upheld their claim, saying that unless they consented no white man had the right to enter their lands. But Congress and President Jackson made no attempt to enforce the decision. In a memorable appeal to Congress, the Cherokees said,

> In truth, our cause is your own. It is the cause of liberty and of justice. It is based upon your own principles, which we have learned from yourselves; for we have gloried to count your Washington and your Jefferson our great teachers. . . . We have practiced their precepts with success. And the result is manifest. The wilderness of forest has given place to comfortable dwellings and cultivated fields. . . . We speak to the representatives of a Christian country; the friends of justice; the patrons of the oppressed. . . . On your kindness, on your humanity, on your compassions, on your benevolence, we rest our hopes.

But those hopes were shattered. More and more settlers resorted to violence to take over Cherokee lands. And the violence was directed not against savages on the warpath but against peaceful farmers and prosperous plantation owners who happened to be Indian. Finally, the U.S. Army was called in, not to protect the Cherokees but to drive them out of their homelands. Soldiers rounded them up—some seventeen thousand men, women, and children—and forced them to march west. Many who tried to defend their homes were shot or bayoneted. Thousands died on the "trail of tears" from disease, ill-treatment, and starvation. Only thirteen thousand survived the ghastly march and reached Oklahoma.

Deeply moved by the tragedy which had struck his people, Sequoyah took an active part in helping to solve the problems raised by the sudden tripling in numbers of the Cherokee community. The six thousand Old Settlers who had established a government to serve their needs now found themselves in a minority. The newcomers had their own chiefs, and were especially devoted to John Ross, who had spearheaded the tribe's efforts to win public support in the United States. The leaders of the Old Settlers, on the other hand, didn't want to give up the control of the government they had set up in Oklahoma. Patient and wise, Sequoyah used his influence to solve the crisis, and finally succeeded in reuniting the divided Cherokee nation. As President of the western Cherokee he signed an act of union which laid the foundation for the adoption of a democratic constitution.

Despite occasional harassment by white outlaws and wild Indian tribes, the Cherokees made rapid progress once again. They expanded the original settlement, taming the wilderness, planting their fields, and building up good herds of cattle. Schools were opened, and a printing press enabled them to print books both in English and Sequoyah's characters. A newspaper, the *Cherokee Advocate,* replacing the earlier *Cherokee Phoenix,* was started; it carried not only news but transcripts of the laws passed by the national council, as well as other information of interest to all Cherokees. With some interruptions, the *Advocate* was published until 1906. At this time Oklahoma was about to become a state and the Cherokee nation was denied the right to exist as a self-governing body.

To his last days, Sequoyah continued to teach and guide

his people wisely. They in turn appreciated this guidance and, as the *Advocate* once wrote, looked upon him as a "remarkable man whose native genius had struck light from darkness—conferred inconceivable blessings upon his people and achieved for his own name imperishable honor." An annual pension was awarded to him by the Cherokee governing council, "in consideration of his great invention."

Many Indians and white men alike journeyed to Sequoyah's home to meet and visit the elderly sage. He wore buckskin leggings and moccasins, and a tunic with a beaded belt at the waist holding a wood-handled knife in a rough leather sheath. His grey hair was covered by a turban, and he smoked a long Indian pipe. "His air," a contemporary remarked, "was altogether what we picture to ourselves of an old Greek philosopher."

An old man, Sequoyah set off with his son Tessee and a few other companions on a long journey southward. He wished to visit a band of Cherokees who many years before had migrated to Mexico—with the probable intention of bringing them his alphabet. During the journey he became ill, but refused to turn back. One night, Indians stole their horses, making Sequoyah's progress even slower. Despite his lame leg and weakened condition, Sequoyah eventually reached Mexico and was warmly welcomed at the Cherokee village. Here, hundreds of miles from home, the great and wise sage died. But unlike Tecumseh's noble vision of a civilized, independent Indian state, Sequoyah's dream did not end with his death. He had given the Cherokees a key to knowledge such as no other tribe possessed. Enduring continued persecutions and hardships, the Cherokees always strove to maintain their ancient heritage while finding a place for themselves within the American nation. Their achievements blazed a trail followed by other tribes, and eventually old enemies were forced to accept them as fellow Americans.

10

Sitting Bull and the Sioux' Last Stand

༄

THE BUFFALO lookouts pawed the ground, sensed an enemy nearby and gave the alarm. Most of the herd stopped grazing, and the big, shaggy brown beasts started milling around, bellowing. On the hilltop, the Sioux hunters sat silently on their horses, waiting for the signal. The *Akicitas*, chosen warriors who acted as the tribe's policemen, kept a wary eye on the young braves who, in their eagerness, might take off too soon and scare the herd away. Finally, the signal was given. The hunters raced swiftly downhill and swooped among the buffaloes with wild yells. Frightened, the huge animals started off at a clumsy trot, slowly gathering speed. Their pounding hooves rumbled like thunder and raised stifling clouds of thick dust enveloping men and beasts.

The Indians rode bareback, bow in hand, with one arm through a cord of twisted hair, lashed around the horse's jaw. They wore only a breechcloth and moccasins, with a quiver made of panther or otter skin strapped to the shoulder. Galloping alongside the intended prey, the hunter aimed at a spot behind the shoulder blade where the sharp, feathered arrow would pierce the thick hide and reach the heart.

This was a good hunting day for the Hunkpapa Sioux.

And it was a great day for young Sitting Bull. He had managed to evade the *Akicitas*, who would have sent him back to wait with the other boys for the end of the hunt. Rushing full speed with the men among the buffaloes, he picked out a big fat bull, drew close to its side, and jerking an arrow from his quiver let it fly at the beast. Snorting, the bull jumped and tried to gore its attacker, but the little horse dodged the charge. The boy clung to its back like a leech, and as the swift pony kept sidestepping the furious animal's horns, he drew another arrow and shot it again. The beast tried a last, frantic rush, but its legs buckled, and its shaggy hulk crashed to the ground. Sitting Bull yelled triumphantly and sprang from his pony. It was his first buffalo—he was a hunter, now.

When the hunt was over dozens of huge carcasses were strewn across the prairie, far and near. In the distance, one could still see the dark backs of a few stragglers in flight. The men started flaying the carcasses and butchering—deftly cutting the sinews to sever the joints and piling the big hunks of meat, which the women would prepare. Someone from time to time sliced a piece of liver, which he ate raw, or cracked a thigh bone and sucked the marrow, as one would an oyster. Finally, the hides and meat were loaded on the horses, and the hunters trekked back to the village.

Sitting Bull had always loved the days that followed a good hunt. There would be plenty of meat, piled high in front of the buffalo-hide lodges—and everyone in the village was welcome to help himself, for the hunter had exclusive right to hide and tongue, but would not dream of not sharing the meat with anyone who needed food. Roasted on a stick over the fire, or boiled, or wrapped in leaves and baked under smoldering coals, fresh buffalo meat was most welcome after the winter diet of dried meat and pemmican, and everybody ate his fill.

Thinly sliced slabs of meat were hung up to dry, and the women went to work on the hides, scraping the flesh off one side, the hair off the other, and then rubbing buffalo brains into them to make them pliant. Sitting Bull had seen this done many times before, but as his mother dressed the hide of his first buffalo he watched every step, waiting eagerly. He couldn't help her—it was woman's work—but soon enough it was his turn. With his father's help, he cut a round piece of tough neck hide, and after shrinking it over the fire, he burned holes around its edge, to lash it to a round wood base. The final touch was the design, revealed in a dream, whose magic power would be even more protective than the shield itself. Sitting Bull designed a black bird with outspread wings in the center and a red band at the edge, with four evenly spaced eagle feathers dangling from it.

When Sitting Bull was young few warriors of his tribe had guns. Most hunted and fought with bows and arrows, shields and lances. The bravest often carried only a coup stick in battle. With this he would touch the enemy and thereby score a coup and win the greatest honor. Sitting Bull was fourteen at the time of his first coup. He had joined a small war party in pursuit of a group of Crow trespassers, and rushing ahead on his fast pony he overtook them, and hit one of them with his carved bone stick. That evening around the campfire, he recounted the story of his coup, according to Indian custom, and the other warriors testified to the truth of his boast, nodding and saying, "That is the way it was," or "I was there, I saw him." As the drums beat and triumphant voices sang a wild victory song, young Sitting Bull swayed and crouched and sprang up in a joyous dance, joining the other warriors.

For a young Sioux, it was a wonderful time to be alive. The Hunkpapas were one branch of the Sioux nation (two others were the Oglala and Brulé Sioux); together, they made up the most powerful Indian nation on the northcentral plains. The Dakotas were their hunting grounds; the name itself was a Sioux word, meaning "allies," and used to describe the whole Sioux family of tribes. To the south of them, wagon trains rolled westward on the Oregon Trail, along the Platte River in Nebraska and Wyoming, but few white pioneers were as yet settling in this part of the country.

Life on the Dakota plains had a magnificent freedom about it, and Sitting Bull's tribe made the most of it. Mounted on their horses, carrying all they owned lashed to a travois made of tepee poles, the Hunkpapas followed the buffalo wherever it roamed. The men hunted; they looked far and near for swift horses to raid, or gallant enemies to fight. They went to battle in war paint, bejeweled with many-colored beads, and on their moccasins, belts, and necklaces they wore porcupine quills. Their horned buffalo caps had a trail of eagle feathers—one for each enemy they had killed—and their magnificent war bonnets were decked with flowing feathers.

Shortly after Sitting Bull's victorious encounter with the Crows—he had now proved himself as both hunter and warrior—the young Sioux brave began his quest for a guiding vision. This too was part of growing up; a man needed dreams and visions to guide him in hunt and battle and everything else that mattered.

Sitting Bull prepared for his quest with the help of a shaman, the medicine man who was at once doctor and priest and magician. The shaman told him many legends of when the earth was young, of how the Sioux nation began, and of the origins of its ancient customs. Then the youth and the shaman went to a hilltop where they built a small sweat lodge using bent poles covered with buffalo hides. Hot stones were placed inside the shelter. Dashing water over them, Sitting Bull took a purifying steam bath, then rushed to splash himself with the cold water of a nearby creek. Naked and

The Sioux celebrated a successful hunt with a triumphant Buffalo Dance

shivering, he was ready for his lonely vigil on the hilltop, with nothing to eat or drink for three long days.

Alone in the vastness of the prairie—at night with the wind sweeping straight down from the cold stars, at dawn facing the bright red sun on the far horizon, and then under the scorching heat of midday—Sitting Bull fought off thoughts of water and food and waited for a vision. And when he felt he could no longer endure the knotted pain in his stomach and his parched, thickly swollen tongue, the vision came. He was one with the earth and the animals and the sun and all men that ever lived; his life was all life. It came and was blindingly clear and then it was gone. But Sitting Bull would not forget it. He had found that "his medicine was good," as the Indians said; he could commune with the mysterious Great Spirit from whom all life came, and thus could count on magic powers.

As the years went by, Sitting Bull's influence grew within his tribe. Because of his bravery in battle and his inspired wisdom he was listened to respectfully in the councils. More and more wagons were rolling through the prairie, and incidents between whites and Indians became more frequent. But Sitting Bull was well aware of the power of the Long Knives, and believed that the pioneers should be left alone— in the hope that his people, in turn, would be left alone in their hunting grounds. Restraining eager warriors angered by the whites' insulting ways and by the diminishing game, Sitting Bull counseled patience. He tried to keep contacts with pioneers and traders to a minimum, although the Indians depended on Fort Laramie and other posts for guns, ammunition, and other goods which had by now become necessities.

In September of 1851, a great treaty council was called by the Superintendent of Indian Affairs, who came from Washington. About ten thousand plains tribesmen gathered

Sitting Bull was highly respected in Indian councils

at Horse Creek, near Fort Laramie. Many groups were traditional enemies who had never met except in combat, and relations were tense. The U.S. government wanted permission to build forts, and Indian guarantees that travel over the Oregon Trail would be safe. In return, it promised to use its soldiers to protect the tribes' rights, and offered to make annual payments in blankets, provisions, and other goods. The Sioux debated these terms, and a majority finally decided in favor of the treaty. But instead of binding all chiefs to the agreement, the American negotiators insisted on having one chief represent them all, and finally appointed the amenable Conquering Bear. This chief signed the treaty but he was never recognized by the Sioux as their real leader. Men like Sitting Bull, Red Cloud, and Spotted Tail were the chiefs who counted, and bypassing them to deal with a "paper chief" like Conquering Bear was not only an insult to the Sioux but an obvious instance of the government's lack of understanding.

This uneasy peace did not last long. Three years later, a few miles from where the solemn treaty council had been held, a bloody incident brought war to the plains. It started when a cow strayed from an emigrant wagon train traveling the Oregon Trail and wandered into a Sioux camp, where it was shot and butchered. Conquering Bear, called into Fort Laramie to answer for what the cow's owner called a theft, offered to pay for the animal. Before an amicable settlement could be reached, a rash young West Pointer decided to settle things his own way. Thirty men with two howitzers set off for the Sioux camp. The impatient officer demanded the man who had killed the cow, and when he did not come forward, the soldiers started firing. Conquering Bear, the whites' own choice as head chief of the Sioux, was the first victim—but shortly afterward, all the soldiers, and the officer who had been so eager to fight, were dead.

Violence bred violence, and as often happens vengeance was wrought upon totally innocent people. There were sudden slaughters in peaceful villages, emigrant families murdered, and wholesale massacres by both sides of defenseless women and children. History repeated on the Dakota plains the cycle of Indian-white relations across the continent. Treaties were quickly broken and followed by fighting, then new and harsher treaties were forced on the unwilling tribes. Finally, in a desperate uprising, the Indians suffered a bloody defeat.

In 1862, the Santee Sioux, who had remained in Minnesota, made their last stand. More than a thousand warriors, led by Little Crow, terrorized the region and plundered and burned scores of farm homes, killing six or seven hundred settlers and tieing up half the troops that Minnesota had put in uniform to fight in the Civil War. Military reprisals cost the lives of a hundred soldiers, but rid the state of its entire Sioux population. The survivors fled west to swell the ranks of the Great Plains tribes, now in almost constant warfare against settlers and government forces.

Sitting Bull had long counseled restraint, but he knew that the Sioux could no longer keep their freedom and their hunting grounds without fighting. He had proved his bravery in battle many times, but his greatest assets as a leader now were his organizing ability, his gift for strategy, and his prestige as a medicine man. He drew on all these gifts to help such war chiefs as Red Cloud and young Crazy Horse resist the white encroachment of Sioux country. Their choice hunting grounds by the Powder River, east of the Big Horn Mountains, were being threatened by the attempted establishment of the Bozeman Trail. This would lead northwest from Fort Laramie to the gold mines of Montana. Sitting Bull's Sioux, joined by groups of Indians from traditionally enemy tribes—Arapaho and Cheyenne—captured government supply trains and pioneers' wagons, seizing precious guns and ammunition. These skirmishes made life impossible for the whites trying to travel and to build forts along the Bozeman Trail.

Repeated efforts to break the Sioux resistance failed before the Indians' skillful tactics. There was Captain William J. Fetterman, for instance, who boasted that with eighty men he would take on the whole Sioux nation. He set out from Fort Phil Kearney with eighty-one soldiers, and was daringly led by Crazy Horse and nine other warriors into a carefully prepared ambush, from which no white men returned.

After several years of fighting, Sitting Bull and the Sioux war chiefs won same important concessions from the U.S. government. Offering peace on Sioux terms, it stipulated that "the country north of the North Platte River and east of . . . the Big Horn Mountains shall be held and considered to be unceded Indian territory, and . . . no white person or persons shall be permitted to settle upon or occupy any portion of the same; or without consent of the Indians . . . to pass through the same." The Bozeman Trail and existing military posts, the treaty specified, would be abandoned. In return, the Sioux were to bury the hatchet and promise not to interfere with the building of the iron trail along the Platte River —the first transcontinental railroad which in 1869 joined Omaha, Nebraska, to the West Coast. Red Cloud signed the treaty, and never again raised arms against the United States; as his prestige among the Indians declined, he was replaced as the main war chief of the Sioux by Crazy Horse, an Oglala who was not yet thirty but already acknowledged, even by his enemies, to be one of the bravest and greatest soldiers of his day. Sitting Bull remained the most influential political leader and medicine man among the Sioux.

The coming of the railroad—and with it swarms of hunters—hastened the disappearance of the buffalo from the plains. Buffalo Bill alone, a one-man commissary for several railroad gangs, claimed to have killed more than four thousand. Many thousands more were slaughtered by other hunters just for the hides, with the wasted carcasses left to rot away. But up in the Black Hills and the Big Horn country there was still enough game, and Sitting Bull—determined to defend Indian territory from white encroachment— was also determined to keep his people from stirring up trouble. For a few years, the Sioux hunted peacefully on their lands. It was the railroad, gold fever, and a flamboyant Indian-fighter named George Armstrong Custer that sent them once more on the warpath, in one of the Great Plains' fiercest wars.

The Northern Pacific was planning to build a railroad line through Indian country, and Custer with his cavalrymen escorted some surveying parties. On an expedition to the Black Hills, he took along gold hunters, and his return set off a gold rush. As prospectors swarmed in, the government started negotiations to buy the land. Failing to reach an agreement, it ordered all hostile Indians to report to the reservations or face military action. The scene was set for a showdown.

In June of 1876, Sitting Bull's Hunkpapas held a Sun Dance. The great chief and medicine man himself danced. Going without food or water for several days, he had dozens of slits cut in the skin of his arms, through which strings were tied; the other end of each string led to a pole, and Sitting Bull danced the grave, simple steps which custom demanded while pulling on the strings until each piece of skin had been torn off. Then he had a vision in which he saw a throng of soldiers falling on his camp. Soon after, scouts reported that the Long Knives were indeed on the march.

The Indians were ready to meet them. In a huge camp by the Little Bighorn River, the Sioux, reinforced by a Cheyenne contingent, had some five thousand warriors, along with about twice as many women, children, and old men. On June 25, General Custer neared the camp with less than seven hundred men. Disregarding the plan which had called for concerted action reinforced by additional U.S. forces, still on their way, Custer decided to attack. His strategy was to circle with five companies to the northern end of the camp, while three companies under Major Reno attacked the southern end. The rest of the men under Captain Benteen would be held in reserve as reinforcements. Custer's plan went wrong from the very beginning. Reno's companies, stopped by Sitting Bull's warriors, were soon in flight; one third of the soldiers died before retreating to a hilltop where Reno dug in, soon reinforced by Benteen. At the other end of the camp, Custer didn't even have a chance to ford the river. Attacked and surrounded, his soldiers broke ranks, and were finally encircled by shooting Indians. Crazy Horse, a lightning streak painted on his face, led the attack yelling, "It's a good day to fight! It's a good day to die!" One by one, the soldiers fell in the desperate hand-to-hand fighting. Finally Custer and all his men, who only an hour earlier had galloped toward the Indian camp to the stirring sound of bugles, lay dead on the field.

Reno and Benteen with the survivors of their companies entrenched themselves on a ridge, and held off the Sioux until Sitting Bull and the other chiefs—faced with the prospect of another major battle against additional troops moving in —decided to withdraw. Custer's defeat shocked the American public. It was announced in the eastern newspapers on July 5, 1876, wounding the pride of a people who were celebrating the one-hundredth anniversary of their nation's independence. The United States poured troops, arms, and supplies into the Sioux country, in a determined drive to break the Indians' resistance. A council between General

An Indian pictograph drawn by Chief Red Horse described
Custer's defeat at the Battle of Little Big Horn

Miles and Sitting Bull failed to produce an agreement: the chief wanted his tribe to be free to live in the Black Hills and Big Horn country as promised by the treaty of 1868; the general insisted that all Sioux must surrender their arms and report at the reservations.

"No Indian that ever lived loved the white man," was Sitting Bull's reply, "and no white man that ever lived loved the Indian. God Almighty made me an Indian—not a reservation Indian—and I don't intend to be one!" A few minutes after the meeting broke up, General Miles ordered his men to fire. Taken by surprise, the Sioux scattered, losing their camp and their whole meat supply.

Without food, hounded by more and more troops, forced to flee through the desperately cold winter, Sitting Bull and his Hunkpapas, in February of 1877, crossed the Canadian border, seeking safety. The other bands of the Sioux who had defeated Custer were dispersed and either killed or forced to the reservations. Crazy Horse held out to the last, but finally had to surrender. Promised a reservation for his people, he put down his arms. Soon after, in prison, he was bayoneted to death. Instead of being given a reservation on their ancestral lands, his people were herded with the other Sioux to a new location on the Missouri River, but on the way some two thousand of them broke away from their guards and managed to join Sitting Bull in Canada.

The gallant Sioux had made their last stand, and lost. Their story from then on was that of captives on reservations—or of exiles and fugitives who would in time be caught and sent to reservations. For awhile, it looked as if Sitting Bull might come to the help of Chief Joseph of the Nez Percés tribe, who managed to fight off U.S. armies during an epic 1300-mile trek from Oregon to the Missouri River and up almost to the Canadian border. But Sitting Bull knew that if he didn't keep the peace, his people could no longer depend on finding safety in Canada. Chief Joseph surrendered: "It is cold and we have no blankets. The little children are freezing to death," he told General Miles as he handed him his gun. "My heart is sick and sad. From where the sun now stands, I will fight no more forever."

In 1881, Sitting Bull himself surrendered to the American commander at Fort Buford. He could no longer hold out in Canada: poverty and hunger, which faced the Sioux now that the buffalo had practically disappeared, accomplished what arms could not. The last band was thus put on the reservation, at Standing Rock, North Dakota. For a brief period, in the mid-1880s, Sitting Bull was taken on a tour of eastern cities and exhibited as General Custer's slayer, then he traveled with Buffalo Bill and his wild west show. But he was soon back at the reservation: "White men talk too much," he commented. "To my ears it's like the noise of waters which man can't stop."

Indian resistance on the Great Plains was at an end. The Apaches in the mountain country of the Southwest had fought for several years in small bands, but even the fierce, ruthless Geronimo had finally been forced to yield. There was no more hope for the Indians, imprisoned in the reservations and stripped of their proud freedom. And yet hope arose again. A Paiute called Wovoka began preaching the return of the Indian world—with the great chiefs and warriors coming back to life, the white men destroyed, and the buffalo once more roaming by the thousands on the plains. This prophet's gospel spread from reservation to reservation, and thousands of Indians took up the chant and ritual dance supposed to bring about by magic the change which warriors could no longer hope to achieve by force of arms. Called the "Ghost Dance" by the whites—because of the white shirts that were supposed to protect dancers even from bullets—this frenzied religious revival worried U.S. authorities and settlers. To them the throbbing tom-toms across the plains meant war dances, and a determined effort was made to stop them.

Sitting Bull played no key role in the movement, but he still was a powerful figure among the Sioux, and U.S. military leaders feared that he might spark an uprising. One night in December, 1890, 140 soldiers and Indian policemen armed with a cannon marched to his village on the Standing Rock Reservation to arrest him. Awakened from his sleep, Sitting Bull resisted, and Indian policemen shot him. Afraid that their turn would come next, some three hundred Hunkpapas fled the village. Cavalrymen overtook them by Wounded Knee Creek, surrounded them, and ordered them to surrender. There were five hundred cavalrymen, facing one hundred Sioux men and two hundred women and children. The Indians surrendered, were disarmed, and their temporary camp in the snow was kept under close watch, with four Hotchkiss machine guns trained on it. A rifle shot rang out—why, no one knows—and the so-called Battle of Wounded Knee began. The troops opened fire. The snow turned red as the Sioux fell: men and women and children, desperately trying to escape the fast drumming of the machine guns. There were no prisoners. And the Indians fought no more.

11

Indian Leaders Today

❧❧

In *The Vanishing American*, novelist Zane Grey tells the sad, moving saga of Nophaie the Indian, a story based on much tragic truth. The impoverished and persecuted tribe Zane Grey portrayed under the name of Nopah was recognizably the Navaho—who a few decades ago faced great misery and suffering, and dramatized for all Americans the plight of many Indians. At the close of the novel, a scene suggested what was, at the time, a widespread belief: the Indians were doomed to extinction.

> It was a magnificent, far-flung sunset, the whole west flaming with intense golden red that spread and paled far into the north. Against this glorious background the Indians were riding away, in dense groups, in long straggling lines, in small parties, down to couples. It was an austere and sad pageant. The broken Indians and the weary mustangs passed slowly out upon the desert. . . . Far to the fore the dark forms, silhouetted against the pure gold of the horizon, began to vanish, as if indeed they had ridden into that beautiful prophetic sky. . . . At last only one Indian was left on the darkening horizon . . . bent in his saddle, a melancholy figure, unreal and strange against that dying sunset— moving on, diminishing, fading, vanishing—vanishing.

There was no hope for Nophaie, thought Zane Grey, no hope for the Nopahs; the American Indians were bound to pass from the scene. But instead of vanishing, during the last thirty years the Indian population in the United States has increased about 60 percent. There are now well over half a million Indians—some estimates put the figure near a million—and although much remains to be done before they all share fully the rights and opportunities of their fellow citizens, a good number of them play a vital part in American life. Many have served in state and national offices, others fill important positions as teachers, jurists, federal employees, doctors. Among the 25,000 Indians who served with distinction in the armed forces during World War II was Major General Clarence Tinker, an Osage, who reorganized U.S. air forces after the attack on Pearl Harbor. One of the greatest all-around American athletes, Jim Thorpe, was a Sauk-Fox. Vice-President Charles Curtis was a descendant of Osage and Kaw chiefs. And one of America's most popular humorists, Will Rogers, used to boast of his Cherokee origins, "My forefathers didn't come over on the *Mayflower*, but they met the boat." And then added, "In fact, they would have showed better judgment if they had not let *your* forefathers land."

Behind the humor, there is the bite of truth. The arrival of white men in America marked the beginning of a long and tragic period in Indian history. Some tribes in the eastern United States disappeared altogether—a few destroyed in the early days of armed clash, others wiped out by disease. Still others, broken and scattered, were assimilated so that only the memory of Indian ancestors is left. But a good many tribal groups managed to keep together, even when removed from their native homeland, like the people of the Five Civilized Tribes who are now in Oklahoma. And several tribes in the West and Southwest—as well as a few small groups in the East—still live where their forefathers did, preserving much of their ancient way of life in Indian-owned reservations.

CULVER PICTURES, INC.

The well-known humorist Will Rogers was proud of his Cherokee origins

Reservations were at first designed to fence in tribes that were in the way of land-hungry pioneers. Today, they are simply tracts of land owned jointly by a group of Indians, each of whom is free to live there or anywhere else he pleases. The Interior Department's Bureau of Indian Affairs is responsible for providing such community services as roads and schools, but it is up to the Indians to develop their reservation's resources and to better their standard of living. This challenge has given rise to a new kind of leader who could not be farther from the traditional image of the Indian chief—and yet needs as much statesmanship as Hiawatha, as much vision as Tecumseh, as much desire to improve his people as Sequoyah.

One doesn't hear much about such men as Paul Jones, for many years the forceful chairman of the Navaho Tribal Council, or about Vice-Chairman Scott Preston, who was trained as a medicine man but has proved to be a most effective twentieth century organizer, shuttling from place to place on the huge Navaho reservation by car and by plane. Yet without such leaders the Navahos would still be living as Zane Grey portrayed them, without a future, without hope.

The Navahos are the largest Indian tribe today, numbering over 85,000. Most of them live on a reservation in Arizona's northwest corner, spilling over into Utah and New Mexico. The reservation covers more than 15,000,000 acres—an area larger than Massachusetts, Rhode Island, and Connecticut put together. This may sound like enough land to support many times their number, but most of it is magnificent—and barren—country where no crops will grow.

The Navahos herded sheep, farmed small plots, and supplemented their meager living from the land with the sale of fine woven blankets and rugs, and silver-and-turquoise jewelry. As their population kept growing, it became increasingly harder to provide even the barest necessities of life. Change had to come, and it was brought by leaders who came from within their own ranks. Chairman Paul Jones was born on the reservation, and attended a government school there for eight years. Continuing his education after grade school was more difficult. He didn't get to high school until he was twenty-two, and he took a job as janitor in order to be able to afford it. He learned the importance of education the hard way, and he has worked hard to make it easily available to the younger generation. The Tribal Council has inaugurated projects designed to develop the reservation's resources and to create jobs for its people. Luck, in the form of some successful oil strikes, helped, but it was wise management that put the income from oil to work on irrigation projects, economic development, and educational opportunities for the whole tribe.

There are other leaders who are doing the same kind of thing for their people elsewhere. In South Dakota, tribal initiative and funds have opened industrial plants on several reservations. Young Robert Burnette of the Rosebud Sioux has masterminded the Tribal Land Enterprise, which in a decade has added nearly 400,000 acres of land to the reservation. Some of it is used for grazing, some leased to stock growers, and a recreation area with campsites, artificial lakes for swimming and boating, and accommodations is bringing in good tourist trade. In one year, reports the dynamic Burnette, the Enterprise's business activities have meant an added income of $250,000 for the Rosebud Sioux.

Outside the reservation, the Indian has all the rights and duties of any other American citizen. Citizenship was granted to many tribes long ago by acts of Congress or through treaties; a special law stating that all Indians born in the United States are citizens was passed belatedly in 1924. Since then, several court decisions and legislative acts have removed the last vestiges of official discrimination. Whether or not he lives on a reservation, the Indian—according to federal law —can vote and run for office, can own property and hold any kind of job, and must serve his country when drafted. This does not mean that discrimination against Indians has disappeared. In some sections of the country, the Indian still faces unequal treatment. It may take the form of segregation in eating places or in housing, or it may mean limited access to jobs. These lingering instances of injustice are painful reminders that there are problems still to be solved before ful-

filling the American dream that "all men are created equal."
On the other hand, progress has been made. And where
there is a large and well-organized group, as in Oklahoma,
Indians exercise real political power.

Elsewhere, individual Indians have achieved high positions
in government not because of a large Indian constituency
but by virtue of their own personal qualifications. In the
spring of 1966, for example, President Johnson appointed as
Commissioner of Indian Affairs Robert La Follette Bennett,
a career civil servant from the state of Wisconsin, who
descends from the Oneidas, one of the five major Iroquois
tribes.

A descendant of another famous tribe, the Sioux, sits in
the U.S. Congress as representative from South Dakota.
Born on the Rosebud Sioux Reservation, Ben Reifel man-
aged to put himself through agricultural school, then took
courses in chemistry and dairy farming at South Dakota
State College. After working many years for the Bureau of
Indian Affairs—with time out for army service in World War
II and for two degrees at Harvard—he decided to run for
Congress. There are only a few thousand Indians in his con-
stituency of 400,000 people, so that Congressman Reifel is
in no way a spokesman for Indian needs and interests alone.
And yet, by heritage and close acquaintance, he is intensely
aware of them, and considers it a part of his duties to further
Indian progress, especially in the field of education.

The same dual role—as representative of both a broad
constituency and a minority in need of special consideration
—has been filled by Indians of other tribes elected to state
legislatures in Alaska, Montana, Nevada, Oklahoma, Washington, and other states, not always those with the heaviest
Indian populations. The largest Indian groups today, besides
the Navahos, are: nearly 150,000 people from the Five Civilized Tribes living in Oklahoma, 75,000 of them Chero-

kees; the Chippewas in Minnesota, Wisconsin, and North
Dakota, nearly 25,000 of whom live on the reservation; the
30,000 Sioux of the Dakotas; the Southwest's Pueblos, numbering about 20,000; the 10,000 Apaches on reservations in
Arizona and New Mexico; and some 8,000 Iroquois in New
York state, part of approximately 50,000 Indians in the eastern states who have not been completely assimilated in the
general population. About 14 out of every 100 Alaskans are
Indians, including nearly 20,000 Eskimos—one of them the
president of the Alaska Senate.

In the professions and in the arts many Indians who were
born and raised on the reservation have achieved positions of
national eminence. Best known among them are perhaps the
Tallchief sisters, whose introduction to the dance was at traditional ceremonies on the Osage reservation in Oklahoma,
and who have become known the world over as ballerinas—
Marjorie with the Paris Opera Ballet and Maria with the
American Ballet Theatre. In the academic world, several Indians are reknowned scholars. There is anthropologist Edward P. Dozier, for instance, who left Santa Clara Pueblo
when he was twelve but has always found time during his
busy and distinguished career to go back and spend some
time with his people. There is Dr. Frederick J. Dockstader,
director of New York's famous Museum of the American Indian, who was eleven when he left the Navaho reservation.
A creative artist recognized by many national awards, he is
a noted scholar as well, and his superbly illustrated study of
Indian art in America is the most comprehensive volume on
the subject. There are several painters who have become
fairly well known—such as Joe Herrera and the Kiowa-Co-
manche Blackbear Bosin—but the most outstanding recent
contribution has probably been that of a Pueblo potter who
never left her native village. María Martínez of San Ildefonso

learned the craft as a child, and later began experimenting in an attempt to recapture the secret of the process which made Pueblo pottery of centuries ago so remarkable. She succeeded, and her work is now included in the collections of major museums here and abroad. Far from keeping her method a jealously guarded trade secret, she taught it to other potters, and thus made San Ildefonso a flourishing craft center.

Success of a very different kind was in store for a young Cherokee who some thirty years ago got a summer job with a big oil company, went on to study engineering, and completed his degree while holding a full-time job with the same company. After steadily climbing the corporate ladder he became its executive vice-president. The career of William W. Keeler of Phillips Petroleum is especially remarkable in that he combined success in business with effective leadership in Indian affairs. A tribal chief of the Cherokee nation in Oklahoma, in 1952 he organized the privately financed Cherokee Foundation for the purpose of helping young people pursue higher education, raising health standards, teaching vocational skills, and preserving the Cherokees' cultural heritage in a permanent museum. Because of Mr. Keeler's active participation in Indian affairs, President Kennedy appointed him chairman of a special task force to evaluate existing federal programs and to make recommendations to the Bureau of Indian Affairs. The Indians, according to the report of Mr. Keeler's task force, "cannot alone decide the kind of future world they will inhabit." But they must be full partners in a concerted effort by all Americans "to help Indians find their way along a new trail—one which leads to equal citizenship, maximum self-sufficiency, and full participation in American life."

An American by right, long before the word America existed, the Indian has been finding his rightful place among the many groups who contributed to the birth of a new nation—as proud of his traditions as the New Englanders, the Swedish Americans of Minnesota, the Polish Americans of Buffalo and Milwaukee, the Italian Americans of Brooklyn and the Napa Valley. The process of adjustment for the Indian has taken longer, because the cultural differences were immeasurably greater and because the long and tragic history of conflict made mutual understanding and cooperation very difficult. But Zane Grey's vanishing Americans are here to stay, and leaders of vision and dedication are working to expand opportunities in every field for their fellow Indians both within and without the reservations.

There is much that Americans can learn from a closer look at their country's complex Indian heritage: The stress on personal qualities over mere personal possessions, for instance, which characterized the Plains Indian—and his generosity, which would never allow another to go hungry if he had any food; the rich imaginative life of the Northwest Indian, his love of beautiful objects—whether for everyday use or designed for a religious or social purpose; the incredible perseverance of the Pueblos stubbornly scraping a living from desert land; the Navahos' harmonious vision of man finding understanding and fulfillment in communion with nature; the community-mindedness which alone has permitted many tribes to survive, by pooling individual efforts and meager resources for the benefit of all.

Frenzied war whoops still fill the air—just before the inevitable rescue at the end of the program—in millions of living rooms throughout the land. They probably can't be stilled, nor is there any reason why they should. The feather-bonneted Indian on the warpath has as sure a place in the American imagination as the fast-shooting cowboy. But an awareness of the Indians as they really were also deserves a place in our culture. They fought for nearly three centuries to save their country and their way of life. Their warfare against the settlers was sometimes cruel, nearly always brave, and more often than we like to remember quite justified. But for all the violence and hatred which divided red and white men over long years of struggle, there is also much which Indians have always had in common with all other Americans: a profoundly democratic view of social organization, which made most southeastern chiefs truly rulers "by consent of the governed"; a deep belief in public discussion and conciliation of views as means to wise government, a foundation of the Iroquois constitution as well as our own; above all, perhaps, a fierce will to be free which made men fight and die, and was expressed by the valiant Chief Joseph of the Nez Percés in words any American should be proud to speak.

Let me be a free man—free to travel, free to stop, free to work, free to trade where I choose, free to choose my own teachers, free to follow the religion of my fathers, free to think and talk and act for myself—and I will obey every law or submit to the penalty. Whenever the white man treats the Indian as they treat each other, then we will have no more wars. We shall all be alike—brothers of one father and one mother, with one sky above us and one country around us, and one government for all.

INDEX

Ahousat tribe, 87
Akicitas, 123, 124
Alderman, 48, 49
Algonkian tribes, 2-3
Algonkins, 2, 3
Amherst, Jeffrey, Baron,
    68, 75-76, 80
Apaches, 7, 54, 59-60, 137, 145
Arapahos, 1, 131
Argall, Captain, 29
Atotarho, 18, 19-20
Awoshonks, 40, 47

Bennett, Robert La Follette, 144
Benteen, Captain Frederick, 134
Blackfoot tribe, 1
Blue Jacket, Chief, 97-98
Bosin, Blackbear, 145
Boston, 82-83, 85, 86, 87, 88
Bouquet, Colonel Henry, 76, 77, 79
Bozeman Trail, 131-132
Braddock, General Edward, 67
Brock, General Isaac, 105-106, 108
Buffalo, 8-10, 123-125, 126, 132-133,
    137
Bureau of Indian Affairs, 141, 144,
    146
Burnette, Robert, 143

Callicum, 85
Cannibalism, 17, 23
Canoes, 17, 24, 82
Canonchet, 45, 46-47
Catherine, 70
Cayugas, 17, 22
Cherokee Advocate, 121
Cherokee Foundation, 146
Cherokee Phoenix, 118, 121
Cherokees, 5, 97, 101, 113-122, 140,
    144, 146

Cheyennes, 1, 131, 133
Chickasaws, 5, 101, 120
Chinook tribe, 11, 87
Chippewa tribe, 18, 70, 71, 74, 79,
    105, 145
Choctaws, 5, 101, 120
Clark, William, 84, 92
Cody, Buffalo Bill, 133, 137
Columbus, Christopher, 14, 17
Comanches, 1, 145
Conquering Bear, 130
Cook, Captain James, 83
Coronado, Francisco de, 6, 28, 50
Cortez, Hernando, 28
Coup, 10, 125
Crazy Horse, 131, 132, 134, 136
Creeks, 5, 97, 101, 108, 116, 120
Crows, 1, 125, 126
Curtis, Charles, 140
Custer, George Armstrong, 133-135,
    137

Dale, Sir Thomas, 30-31, 33
Dalyell, Captain, 76-77
Dances, 7, 85; Calumet (Ottawa),
    63; Ghost (Sioux), 137-138; Sun
    (Sioux), 133
Degandawida, 18, 19, 22-23
Delawares, 23, 68, 71, 74, 75, 77,
    79
Detroit, *see* Fort Detroit
Dockstader, Dr. Frederick J., 145
Dozier, Edward P., 145

Echachet tribe, 90-91
Eskimos, 145

Fallen Timbers, Battle of, 97-98
Fetterman, Captain William, 132
Five Civilized Tribes, 5, 6, 140, 144

Five Nations, *see* Great Peace
Fort Detroit, 63, 64, 67, 68, 71, 72-74, 76, 81, 106
Fort Wayne, Treaty of, 100
Franklin, Benjamin, 13
French and Indian War, 67

Galloway, Rebecca, 98-99
Geronimo, 137
Ghent, Treaty of, 111
Ghost Dance, *see* Dances
Gladwin, Major Henry, 63, 69-70, 71, 76, 78-79
Government of Indian tribes, 5, 10, 13, 20, 114
Great Peace, 3, 13, 14, 17, 19-24
Greenville, Treaty of, 98
Grey, Zane, 139, 142, 147
Guess, George, *see* Sequoyah

Harrison, William Henry, 93-96, 99-104, 108, 109-111
Harvard University, 144
Hennepin, Father Louis, 20
Heritage of American Indian, 12-15, 147
Herrera, Joe, 145
Hiawatha, 3, 14, 18-24
Hopis, 55
Horses, 1, 38, 51, 126
Horseshoe Bend, Battle of, 116
Hull, General William, 104-05
Huron tribe, 64, 68, 71, 77, 79

Iowa tribe, 101
Iroquois, 3-4, 16-24, 45, 57, 66, 67, 68, 144, 145
Iroquois League, *see* Great Peace

Jackson, Andrew, 108, 116, 120
Jamestown Colony, 26, 27, 28, 29, 32-33
Jamestown massacre (Great Massacre of 1622), 32
Jefferson, Thomas, 92
Jewitt, John, 86, 90, 92
Johnson, Lyndon B., 144
Johnson, Sir William, 80
Jolly, Chief, 116
Jones, Paul, 142
Joseph, Chief, 136, 137, 148
Juan, 55-56

Kachinas, 50
Kaw tribe, 140
Keeler, William W., 146
Kendrick, John, 84
Kennedy, John F., 146
Kickapoo tribe, 74
King, Charles Bird, 118
King George's War (1744-1748), 67
Kiowas, 145
Kiva, 50
Klayoquot tribe, 87
Kwakiutl tribe, 11
Kyuquot tribe, 87

Lacrosse, 33, 63, 74
La Salle, Robert, Sieur de, 20
Laulewasika, *see* The Prophet
Lewis, Meriwether, 84, 92
Little Crow, 131
Longhouse, 3, 12, 17, 20, 66
Longfellow, Henry Wadsworth, 18
Lydia, 92

Madison, James, 102
Mandan, 1
Maquinna, 82-92
Martínez, María, 145-146
Mascouten tribe, 74
Masks, 84, 85, 92
Massasoit, 14, 35, 37-38, 39
Matoonas, 48
Meares, John, 84
Metacom, *see* Philip of Pokanoket
Miamis, 23, 68, 71
Michilimackinac, Fort, massacre at, 74
Miles, General Nelson A., 136, 137
Mingo tribe, 71
Mohawks, 17, 18, 22, 45
Mohegan tribe, 42, 47, 48
Mohican tribe, 101
Monacan tribe, 28
Muchalat tribe, 87

Narragansett tribe, 35, 40, 45, 46-47, 101
Navahos, 7-8, 59-60, 139, 142
Nez Percés tribe, 136, 148
Nipmuck tribe, 40, 42, 48
Nootka tribe, 11, 82-92

Oñate, Juan de, 51
Oneida tribe, 17, 22, 144
Onondaga tribe, 17, 18, 20, 22, 23
Opekankano, 25
Oregon Trail, 126, 130
Osage tribe, 101, 140, 145
Otermín, Antonio de, 55-58, 59, 60
Ottawa tribe, 63, 64, 66, 67, 68-70, 71, 74, 105

Paiute tribe, 137
Pemaquid tribe, 36
Peoria tribe, 80
Pequot tribe, 47, 101
Philip of Pokanoket, 35-49
Pizarro, Francisco, 28
Plymouth Colony, 36-40, 46
Pocahontas, 2, 27, 29-32, 33, 34
Pocasset tribe, 40, 42, 46, 48
Pokanoket, 36, 40, 41, 48
Pontiac, 63-81
Popé, 50, 52, 54, 55, 57, 58-59, 60, 62
Potawatomi tribe, 64, 68, 71
Potlatch, 87-88
Potomac tribe, 29
Powhatan, 2, 14, 25-33
Preston, Scott, 142
Proctor, General Henry A., 108-111
Prophet, The, 99-100, 102, 104
Pueblo tribes, 1, 7, 13, 14, 51-62, 145; Pecos, 54; Picuris, 54, 56; Taos, 54, 55, 56; Tesuque, 54; Tewa, 52, 54, 56; Yugue-Yunque, 54

Red Cloud, 130, 131, 132
Reifel, Ben, 144
Reno, Major Marcus A., 134
Reservations, 137, 138, 140, 141, 142, 143, 144, 145
Revolutionary War, 4, 96, 97
River Raisin Massacre, 108
Rogers, Will, 140
Rolfe, John, 30, 32, 33
Ross, John, 121
Rousseau, Jean Jacques, 4

Sakonnet tribe, 40, 47, 48
Salter, Captain, 83, 85
Samoset, 36-37
San Ildefonso Pueblo, 145-146

Santa Clara Pueblo, 145
Santa Fe, 51, 52, 54, 55, 56-58, 62
Satsatsoksis, 88
Sauk-Fox, 140
Seminole tribe, 5, 101, 108
Senecas, 17, 22, 68, 74, 79
Sequoyah, 113-122, 142
Seven Years' War, 67
Shawnee tribe, 23, 68, 74, 75, 77, 79, 93-96, 101
Shoshoni tribe, 10
Sioux, 1, 14, 123-138, 143, 144, 145; Hunkpapa, 123, 125-126, 133, 136, 138; Oglala, 132; Santee, 131
Sitting Bull, 14, 124-138
Slaves, 44, 90, 91, 92, 114
Smith, Captain John, 26-27, 28-29
Spotted Tail, 130
Squanto, 38
Standing Rock Reservation, North Dakota, 137, 138

"Talking leaves," 113-115, 118
Tallchief, Maria and Marjorie, 145
Tecumseh, 93-112, 122, 142
Tepees, 124, 126
Thames, Battle of the, 110-111
Thompson (sailmaker), 86, 88, 92
Thorpe, Jim, 140
Tinker, Major General Clarence, 140
Tippecanoe, Battle of, 102-103
Tlingit, 11
Tobacco, 33
Totem pole, 12
"Trail of Tears," 121
Travois, 126
Tribal Land Enterprise, 143
Tuscarora tribe, 22

Ute tribe, 10

Vanishing American, The, 139
Vargas, Diego de, 60
Vision quest, 126-128

Wampanoag tribe, 35-36, 37-49
Wampum, 23, 24, 39, 70
Wamsutta, 38
War of 1812, 4
Washington, George, 4, 67
Wayne, General Anthony, 98

Wea tribe, 74
Weapons, 16, 90, 125
Weetamoo, 40, 42, 45, 46, 48
Weremocomoco, 27, 28, 30
Whaling, 91
Wigwams, 2, 16, 17
Winnebago tribe, 102

Wolfe, Chief, 71
Wounded Knee Creek, South
    Dakota, massacre at, 138
Wovoka, 137
Wyandot tribe, 110

Zuñi, 55